The Second Revised Edition

The Ancient

Mysteries of

Melchizedek

by Melchizedek Y. Lewis (a.k.a. Yohanan Lewis)

WAR IN HEAVEN SPECIAL EDITION

March 2006

Revised Edition June 1997

First Edition September 1993

ISBN NO.: 0-9665426-1-4

DISTRIBUTED BY:

**AFRICAN WORLD BOOKS
2217 PENNSYLVANIA AVENUE
BALTIMORE, MD 21217**

TELEPHONE: 410-383-2006

All scriptural quotations used in this book were taken from the HOLY NAME BIBLE containing The Holy Name Version of THE OLD AND NEW TESTAMENTS.

Critically compared with ancient authorities and various manuscripts. Revised by A. B. Traina

TABLE OF CONTENTS:

Acknowledgments

This book is dedicated to those who are seeking the greatest part of themselves -- the divine, the unlimited, the audacious and the loving.

Many thanks to my daughter Talia Lewis for the help and support she's given by contributing the art illustrations to this project. May all that she set her hands to do prosper throughout her life.

This is in loving remembrance of my late wife, Malkiyah Lewis, for her love and support and great contribution to the first Edition of this book.

Heartfelt thanks to my editing staff for their diligent work in translations and editing of the revised editions of this work.

Melchizedek Y. Lewis

INTRODUCTION

I am a student of truth, and in my search for a deeper and more profound understanding of life, I have experienced many teachers and teachings, all of which have aided my spiritual growth in some way; however, I was always left with the feeling that something essential was missing from the teaching I was receiving. It was with the introduction of the original and Holy Name of the Creator of the Heavens and the Earth and all that is within it - Yahweh - and the original and Holy Name of His Son - Yahoshua the Messiah the physical manifestation of Yahweh - that my search ended; it was not an end of the search for truth, but an end of the search for a path I would follow which could lead to the greatest expression of my Higher Self. That introduction came from the man who would later be my husband and very best friend, Melchizedek Levi, who presented the Name and all the mysteries attached to it with power, command, and authority. I have had many spiritual teachers but my husband is the greatest of them all. Not only are his words a manifestation of power, but also his life is a testimony of Yahoshua's words:

> *"Ye have heard that it hath been said, Thou shall love thy neighbor and hate thine enemy. But I say unto you, love your enemies, bless them that curse you, do good to them that persecute you, and pray for them who despitefully use you."*
>
> *Matt. 5:43-44*

I have been a humble and devoted student, and it has been my great pleasure to edit this very important book, which was worked on under challenging conditions during our two year stay in Nigeria, West Africa. In his School for the Prophets, where the mysteries of the Holy Scriptures and the power of the Holy Name is taught, I was a part of and a witness to the wonderful transformations that can take place when one understands and follows the teachings put forth in this book.

The concept, *'As it is above (heaven), so it is below (on earth),'* is a maxim that recurs throughout this work. With a deeper understanding of the Four Worlds, we are guided to understand that with faith, confidence, and a proven *method*, we can tap into the highest and most subtle world and draw from it that which we deeply desire. This world is the essence of each and every one of us.

We are approaching the end of an age, `the Last Days' as some call it. This is the Age of Grace, in which mankind, though undeserving, is receiving unmerited favor from the Almighty Creator. We have been given the final opportunity to embrace a way of living which is in accord with the instructions established by the Almighty Creator and due to the Creators mercy we have also been given an opportunity to save ourselves from the period of destruction which will cover the earth before the new age. This is the age in which the Millennium Kingdom will be established.

It is written that `we are Elohim - Almighty Creators - yet we die like earthly men' because we have forgotten our true birthright; we have forgotten that we have been formed and fashioned in the image and likeness of Yahweh.

This book is an attempt to prepare those who have ears to hear for the Millennium Kingdom - the period or age of peace and joy where there will be no disease of body, mind or spirit. This is hard to imagine for some but can *you* stretch your spiritual eye to imagine such a time? It will be a time when we will again walk righteously as Elohim - Almighty Creators. It has been prophesied by the ancient ones and it *will* be a reality.

The information given here is a sincere love offering. . .

Much of the information in this text has the Bible as it's source - originally translated from ancient Hebrew. Many errors have been made in the translation of the great Hebrew Scriptures; some have tried to interpret the Bible in what they call literal translation, but the Hebrew language cannot be translated into a classical language. It is an idiomatic language, and one Hebrew word may have from three to ten different meanings and sometimes it has opposite meanings. Therefore, whole thoughts must be translated.

As you read this text, you will notice that the commonly used names of Lord and God, have been replaced with the Hebrew names Yahweh and Elohim. Jesus and Christ have been replaced with the Hebrew name Yahoshua the Messiah. These original names have been blotted from the consciousness of many people, but they are words of power and must be incorporated into spiritual language again.

By far, the most egregious error committed by the translators is the elimination of heaven's revealed name of the Most High Power, Yahweh, and the name of His son, Yahoshua the Messiah, and substituting the names of the local deities of the nations among whom they dwelt. Yahweh was substituted with the Babylonian deity, Baal, and the Canaanite deity, Adonai, both corresponding to the English word, Lord. The Assyrian deity, `Gawd' or `God' in English, has substituted Elohim, the Almighty Creator. The name of the Son, Yahoshua, has been substituted by Jesus, Iesus and Ea-Zeus (Healing) Zeus, or Zeus the sky god, and Zeus Soter, meaning Zeus the Savior.[1]

The names Lord, God, Jesus and Christ in no way represent the true and holy meaning of the Names that were revealed from the heavenly realms to the prophets of old (see Chapter on the Tetragrammaton). By employing these names, people are unknowingly using the names of deities over the sacred names used in the ancient days, and ascribing the holy attributes of the Almighty Creator to pagan deities.

Scholars and those who are interested in their personal transformation enough to rectify the harm done by this substitution must do further reading and research.

The Sacred Name of the Almighty Creator, Yahweh, is the only name by which He was known in the entire scriptures. Although the traditional English translation of the Bible does not reveal this truth, the terms which are so popular today ('Lord,' 'God' and 'Jesus') cannot be found anywhere in the original Hebrew text of the Bible. Even the translators of the modern Hebrew biblical texts have incorrectly referenced the Creator's Name as 'Yahwah' instead of Yahweh, in order that man would not know nor pronounce the Holy Name of Yahweh. This trend was initiated by the Masoretic Jews, who changed the vowels of the Holy Name to keep the correct pronunciation of the Holy Name concealed:

"יהוה ("Yahweh," is the proper name of God) is written either -יהוה - pointed with the vowels of אדוני ('Adonai'- "Lord"), or as - יהוה - pointed with the vowels of אלוהים (Elohim), and is to be pronounced as the word whose vowels it borrows. This deliberate mispointing was an effort by the scribes to make the name of God (Yahweh) unpronounceable and thus to keep it from being taken in vain (Exodus 20.7; Leviticus 24.11). This device was misinterpreted in 1520 by one Galatinus who mixed the vowels of אדוני ('Adonai') with the consonants of יהוה (Yahweh), thus producing the hybrid form Jehovah, which has remained with us to this day."[2]

Despite the presumed intent of the Masoretic Scribes, through falsifying the Holy Name of Yahweh, they have done the very thing that Yahweh commanded man not to do, which was to destroy His Name through 'falsehood' or 'vanity.' *(See Exodus 20.7 and footnote, p.12).*

Also, the Sacred Name of the Messiah, Yahoshua, is the only name by which he was known to his disciples and the people of his day. His name is composed of two parts Yah-Hoshua, which means Yah or Yahweh (the Creator), and Hoshua - the Savior.'

> *"And she shall bring forth a Son, and thou shall call his name Yahoshua: for He shall save His people from their sins." Matthew 1:21*

The scriptures are specific and leave no doubt about the importance of His name and our responsibilities concerning it:

> *"I am Yahweh: that is My Name, and My glory will I not give to another (name) neither my praise to graven images." Is. 42.8*

> *"How long shall it be in the heart of the prophets that prophesy lies? Yea, they are prophets of the deceit of their own hearts; which think to cause my people to forget My Name - as their fathers have forgotten My Name for Baal (Lord). Jeremiah 23.26-27*

> *"And I have declared unto them Thy Name and will declare it." John 17.26*

There is power in the Name; there is power in the source; there is power in the truth. Returning to the original is important if we are to follow the commands given us by the Almighty Creator, Yahweh Elohim: "Thou shall not take away the Name of Yahweh thy Elohim 'to bring it to naught,' for Yahweh will not hold him guiltless that takes away His Name 'to bring it to naught*." Exodus 20.7.

It is our intention in this work to make more available to seekers of truth, the power embodied in the ancient and Holy Names of the Almighty Creator - Yahweh, and His Son - Yahoshua the Messiah. He was the first High Priest

---

*'To bring to naught': In most King James Translations of the Bible, this word usually appears as 'to take in vain.' The word in the original Hebrew text is actually two words 'heesah' (הישא) ,'to destroy, ruin, devastate, cause to crash into ruins,' and 'shava' (שוע), meaning 'a lie, falsehood; nothingness, vanity, worthlessness.'

11

after the Order of Melchizedek, who has left us specific methods to employ so that like him, we may walk the earth as Elohim - Almighty Creators.

> *"Verily, verily, I say unto you, he that*
> *believeth on Me, the works that I do shall he*
> *do also; and greater works than these shall*
> *he do; because I go unto My Father." John*
> *14.12.*

Hebrew is the language of creation, therefore we use Hebrew names and terms rather than the English, which historically has been proven to fall short in expressing powerful spiritual concepts.

Now we are about to take you on a spiritual journey into the heights and depths of ancient wisdom and spiritual power. We implore you to approach this information with an open, searching, and questioning mind. Some of the information here may be new; some may seem strange to you, but growth requires a mind that pierces through to the core of new ideas before it negates them as useless:

> *"No man putteth a piece of new cloth into*
> *an old garment, for that which is put in to*
> *fill it up taketh from the garment and the*
> *tear is made worse. Neither do men put new*
> *wine into old skins; else the skins burst, and*
> *the wine runneth out, and the skins perish:*
> *but they put new wine into new skins, and*
> *both are preserved. Matt. 9.16-17.*

Malkiyah Levi

Therefore, this phrase can be more correctly translated as 'destroy through falsehood or vanity' or, fully, 'thou shalt not destroy the name of Yahweh your Strong One through falsehood or vanity.'

TO THE READER

He who seeks truth, and is determined to uncover and master the secrets of the universe for himself, is treading a path beset with many pitfalls, danger and illusions. The weakest points in his character, the tiniest chinks in his armor, will be cunningly and subtly attacked.

Honesty and sincerity are the keys that will enable him to reach and to recognize truth; plain honesty about himself, his purpose and other people.

Mainly two things sidetrack seekers of truth: a love of sensationalism and laziness (not studying), both of which undermine their honesty. You must know that sensationalism (emotional excitement) is to the mind what sexual overindulgence is to the body. Even religious emotion can be a type of mental sensuality, and therefore unbalancing.

The capacity to understand truth is the greatest attribute that the mind can cultivate. The mind must be trained (through discipline) just like a muscle, to cope with certain ideas and perceptions, and this very training enlarges and expands the capacity to understand still more. After a period of such training and discipline, one can explain to an intelligent person something that he would have been quite incapable of visualizing at the beginning of it.

The first effort of the seeker, then must be to avoid laziness (lack of study) and to love honesty and discipline. When once we are attuned to this ideal we will be able to distinguish a wise and good person from one who is not, thereby avoiding a number of disillusions and pitfalls.

The truly wise person, usually passes unnoticed among all those who are not seeking the same purity of motive, the same vibration as his own. He is sometimes very cleverly made to look like he has undue problems or weaknesses by those who are fakers themselves or who really don't understand.

The faker or one who pretends to serve the Creator and man is usually very attractive to others. He has a strong character, and often arouses extreme love and devotion in the people around him. Anything unbalanced in his character is deemed by his emotionally minded followers as his 'little ways.'

A person who poses as a highly evolved being, a teacher of others, and yet has the same habits and weaknesses and lack of sensitivity; who does not understand that to serve is to exist, makes a tremendously strong appeal because his achievements apparently need little discipline and rigidity. For that reason his followers are eager to adore his character and he allows, against the law, such adoration, thereby feeding his own vanity and their attachment to physical form. They are not encouraged to think, but to believe blindly what he teaches them; the teacher once this blindness is established, encounters no spur of criticism or judgment to keep him to the giving of his best. If so, the one making the accusation is made to look like they're the problem. So the community that he pretends to serve soon becomes a sham and true divine intellect retires; thus he remains a 'big fish in a little pond.'

The inevitable result of this situation is that a hypnotic condition arises, due first to the teacher's desperate desire to keep his followers attention fixed only upon himself so that they will not discover that they too can think and thereby cease to contribute to his personal sustenance; and second to his followers - to give themselves up to the lazy, emotional state of adoring a physical character, believing in wonders without the use of true divine intellect, and flattering themselves with the importance of possessing a 'great teacher.'

This situation is frequently encountered. The combination of character worship, emotional, sensual and sexual indulgence of all kinds, fraudulence, destructiveness, and disconnection of the Divine Mind, makes it an ambitious imitation of the real thing and deterioration is eminent.

The use of the developed mind power or divine intellect for the wrong purpose, is satanic. Any desire for the possession of others for either good or bad reasons is an act contrary to the great Love that stipulates complete free will. The moment such power is established, we have a state of hypnotism, in slight or intense form. Thus, a group of non-thinking, zombie-like followers results.

Navi Ben Israel

"Everywhere I've gone in the world, I've seen this condition. He who reads and believes everything he reads, need not read, for he becomes a fool. But he who reads and proves what he reads to be true or false, is to be wise. Read this work, and prove the words therein."

The Author

Food for Thought

> "Reprove not a scorner, lest he hate thee; rebuke a wise man and he will love thee." Pr. 9.8

> "Give instruction to a wise man, and he will be yet wiser; teach a just man and he will increase in learning." Pr. 9.9

> "The fear of Yahweh is the beginning of wisdom and the knowledge of the holy is understanding." Pr. 9.10

> "For by me thy days shall be multiplied, and the years of thy life shall be increased." Pr. 9.11

> "Love not sleep, lest thou come to poverty; open thine eyes, and thou shalt be satisfied with bread." Pr. 20.13.

Key Terms:

Belial (בל'אל) = Lord of Lies and Deception

The Devil, is written in the Hebrew text as Shayde (שד), singular, or Shaydeem (שדים), plural which means devil, demon or evil spirit; from the verb Shadad (שדד), to deal violently with despoil, devastate, ruin, create havoc.

The Dragon is Tanin (תנן), one who devours, howls and laments

Elohim - Powers (the plural of El); alternate meaning is *an object of fear* from the title *Eloha**; it is used to refer to YHWH; judges, rulers; divine ones (superhuman beings or powers, the Creator Sons and the Created Sons of YHWH and angels); deities (idols of the nations)**Melkiresha** (מלכירשע) = My King is Wickedness

Satan, from the verb Satan (שתן) which means to turn aside, stray, be seduced, to bear a grudge have animosity against, take persistent assaults on someone/something. The noun is Satan (שתן), Who is the adversary, one who is remote – especially from truth and from the mercy of Yahweh in general – a personal, or national accuser.

Serpent is Nahash (נפש) in the Hebrew script, used to identify a deadly enemy or oppressor, who is perniciousness in unrighteousness, crafty, a tempter, a symbol of world power, one who practices divination, observe signs, divines by omens, enchantment, lust, harlotry, a magician, one who uses black magic

Nebadon –

Edentia -

Satania -

Lanonondek -

Creator Sons – Elohim, the 7 Spirits of Yahweh

Notes from The Editor:

THE AGES OF AGES & ELOHIM

The Universal Father & The Creator Sons

The Universal Father is the El Elyon (The Power Over All Creative Powers) of all creation, the First Source and Center of all things and beings. First think of El Elyon the Universal Father, as Creator, then as Controller, and lastly as an Infinite Upholder. All the Powers who were created by El Elyon were One Unity (Achad) with Him. This Unity of the Powers of Yahweh, His Created Sons who He gave the power to create, were called Elohim. In perfect Unity, Yahweh is Elohim.

Millions upon millions of Ages ago, in the world of pure existence (the Atsilutic World), El Elyon, The Universal Father and Creator, who is spirit and creative light, willed to be and created himself from the intangible to the tangible, from the unknown to the known, from the invisible to the visible creation. (Col. 1:16-19, John 4:24). In the creative process, El Elyon named Himself according to his nature, YAHWEH - The Self Existing One, Who Wills all things to be.

The Universal Father, who is pure existence (Spirit), reproduced Himself, creating his first and only begotten son.

Son = (בן pronounced *Bain*) = a prime root from the verb *Banah*, which means *to build, (lit. and fig.) to obtain children, to repair or set up.* Begotten = 1) to procreate as the father 2) to produce as an effective cause

The Son or Bain, was a master builder, as well, and called himself Michael (He who is like The Power). (John1:1-14). Michael was given the power and authority

20

to create, for he is the tangible image of the Father's Spirit and son in one Unity. Yahweh, through Michael, continued his multifaceted creation of light from the unknown to the known creation by duplicating himself and calling him Gabriel (the great power). Then the universal mandate of creation went out: *"let us create in our own image"* (Gen. 1:26). There were created 7 (seven) Creator Sons known as the seven spirits of Yahweh Elohim (Almighty Creators) (Rev. 4:5). These Creator Sons were given instructions to create universes and other celestial beings after their image, and they would be rulers of their creation in the likeness of the Universal Father, Yahweh El Elyon.

These are the names of the major seven Creator Sons or Elohim of El Elyon, the chief ruler of whom is Michael -the only begotten son of Yahweh El Elyon:

Creator Sons - The Elohim

(1) Michael (2) Gabriel (3) Father Melchizedek (4) Malachim (5) Auphanim (6) Bright and Morning star and (7) Cherubim. There are thousands other Creator Sons and orders of celestial beings that were created.

Just to name a few there are: Supernapim, Seconaphim, Tertiaphim Omniaphim, Seraphim, Sanobim, Ishim, Sons of Melchizedek, Midway Creatures, Vorondadeks, Lanonandeks, Brilliant Evening Stars, Archangels, Life Carriers, Beni Elohim, Magisterial Sons, Chaschmalim, Aralim.

Each one of these Creator Sons (Elohim) was given a mandate that they would have to bestow themselves seven times in the likeness of the created worlds to understand how to rule in righteousness and to know what his creation has to experience. Michael chose the earth for his seventh bestowal, about which it was revealed to the holy prophets before his arrival that he would manifest himself as Yahoshua the Messiah.

The following represents excerpts, from Isaiah the prophet written in the Lost Writings found in the Pseudopigrapha, entitled *The Ascension of Isaiah The Prophet* regarding the existence of Yahoshua the Messiah and the fate of unbelievers:

The Ascension of Isaiah The Prophet

The Martyrdom of Isaiah and Yahoshua the Messiah:

Hezekiah summons Manasseh

In the twenty-sixth year of his reign Hezekiah king of Judah summoned Manasseh his son, for he was his only son. He summoned him in the presence of Isaiah, the son of Amoz, the prophet, and in the presence of Josab the son of Isaiah, in order to hand over to him the words of righteousness, which the king himself had seen, And (the words concerning) the eternal judgments, and the torments of Gehenna, and the prince of this world, and his angels, and his authorities, and his powers, And the words concerning faith in the Beloved which he himself had seen in the fifteenth year of his reign during his sickness. And he handed to him the written words which Samnas the secretary had written out, and also those which Isaiah the son of Amoz had given to him, and to the prophets also, that they might write out and store up with him what he himself had seen in the house of the king concerning the judgment of the angels and concerning the destruction of this world, and concerning the robes of the righteous and their going out, and concerning their transformation and the persecution and ascension of the beloved. In the twentieth year of the reign of Hezekiah Isaiah had seen the words of this prophecy and had handed them to Josab his son. And while (Hezekiah) was giving his commands, with Josab the son of Isaiah standing by, Isaiah said to Hezekiah the king, and not only in the presence of Manasseh did he say (it) to him, *"As YAHWEH lives whose name has not been transmitted to this world and as the Beloved of my YAHWEH lives, and as the spirit which speaks in me lives, all these commands and these words will have no effect on Manasseh your son, and through the deeds of his hands, tormented in body I will depart. And Sammael Malkira will serve Manasseh and will do everything he wishes, and he will be a follower of Beliar rather than of me. He will cause many in Jerusalem and Judah to desert the true faith, and Beliar will dwell in Manasseh and by his hands I will be sawed in half.*" And when Hezekiah heard these words, he wept very bitterly, and tore his robes, and threw earth on his head, and fell on his face. And Isaiah said to him, *"Sammael's plan against Manasseh is complete; there will be no benefit to you from this day."* And Hezekiah thought in his heart that he would kill Manasseh his son, But Isaiah said to Hezekiah, *"The Beloved has made your plan ineffective, and the thought of your heart will not come about; for with this calling have I been called, and the inheritance of the Beloved will I inherit."*

And it came about that after Hezekiah had died, and Manasseh had become king, (Manasseh) did not remember the commands of Hezekiah his father, but forgot them; and Sammael dwelt in Manasseh and clung closely to him. And Manasseh abandoned the service of the ELOHIM of his father, and he served Satan, and his angels and his powers. And he turned his father's house, which had been in the presence of Hezekiah, away from the words of wisdom and the service of YAHWEH. Manasseh turned them away so that they served Beliar; for the angel of iniquity who rules this world is Beliar, whose name is Matanbukus. And he rejoiced over Jerusalem because of Manasseh, [nd he strengthened him] in causing apostasy, and in the iniquity which was disseminated in Jerusalem. And sorcery and magic, augury and divination, fornication and adultery, and the persecution of the righteous increased through Manasseh, and through Belkira, and through Tobiah the Canaanite, and through John of Anathoth, and through Zaliq Neway. And the rest of the acts, behold they are written in the book of the kings of Judah and Israel.

Isaiah withdraws from Jerusalem
And when Isaiah the son of Amoz saw the great iniquity which was being committed in Jerusalem, and the service of Satan and this wantonness, he withdrew from Jerusalem and dwelt in Bethlehem of Judah. And there also was great iniquity; and he withdrew from Bethlehem and dwelt on a mountain in a desert place. And Micah the prophet, and the aged Ananias, and Joel, and Habakkuk, and Josab his son, and many of the faithful who believed in the ascension into heaven, withdrew and dwelt on the mountain. All of them were clothed in sackcloth and all of them were prophets; they had nothing with them, but were destitute, and they all lamented bitterly over the going astray of Israel. And they had nothing to eat except wild herbs (which) they gathered from the mountains, and when they had cooked (them), they

ate them with Isaiah the prophet. And they dwelt on the mountains and on the hills for two years of days.

The story of Zedekiah and Micaiah

And after this, while they were in the desert, there was a certain man in Samaria named Belkira, of the family of Zedekiah the son of Chenaanah, the false prophet, whose dwelling (was) in Bethlehem. And Zedekiah the son of Chenaanah, who was the brother of his father, was the teacher in the days of Ahab, king of Israel, of the four hundred prophets of Baal. And he struck and abused Micaiah, the son of Amida, the prophet. And Ahab abused him and Micaiah was thrown into prison with Zedekiah the prophet; they were with Ahaziah the son of Alamerem Balalaaw. And Elijah the prophet from Tishbe in Gilead reproved Ahaziah and Samaria and he prophesied concerning Ahaziah that he would die on his bed of sickness, [and] Samaria would be given into the hand of Shalmaneser, because he had killed the prophets of YAHWEH. And when the false prophets who (were) with Ahaziah the son of Ahab and their teacher Jalerias from mount Joel heard-now he was a brother of Zedekiah- when they heard, they persuaded Ahaziah the king of Aguaron and [killed] Micaiah.

Isaiah is accused

And Belkira discovered and saw the place of Isaiah and of the prophets who were with him, for he himself dwelt in the district of Bethlehem, and he was a follower of Manasseh. And he prophesied lies in Jerusalem and there were many from Jerusalem who joined with him, but he himself was from Samaria. And it came about, when Shalmaneser the king of Assyria came and captured Samaria, and took the nine tribes into captivity and led them to the provinces of the Medes and the rivers of Gozan, this youth escaped and came to Jerusalem in the days of Hezekiah king of Judah, but he did not walk in the ways of his Samaritan father because he feared Hezekiah. And he was found in the days of Hezekiah speaking words of iniquity in Jerusalem. And the servants of Hezekiah accused him, and he escaped to the district of Bethlehem and persuaded.... And Belkira accused Isaiah and the prophets who (were) with him, saying, *"Isaiah and the prophets who (are) with him prophesy against Jerusalem and against the cities of Judah that they will be laid waste, and also (against) Benjamin that it will go into captivity, and also against you O king, that you will go (bound) with hooks and chains of iron. But they prophesy lies against Israel and Judah."* And Isaiah himself has said, *'I see more than Moses the prophet.'* Moses said, *'There is no man who can see YAHWEH and live.'* But Isaiah has said, *'I have seen YAHWEH, and behold I am alive.' Know, therefore, O king, that they (are) false prophets. And He has called Jerusalem Sodom, and the princes of Judah and Jerusalem He has declared (to be) the people of Gomorrah."* And he brought many accusations against Isaiah and the prophets before Manasseh. But Beliar dwelt in the heart of Manesseh and in the heart of the Princes of Judah and Benjamin, and of the eunuchs, and of the king's counselors. And the words of Belkira pleased him very much, and he sent and seized Isaiah.

A prophecy about the Beloved and the Church

For Beliar was very angry with Isaiah because of the vision and Because of the exposure with which he had exposed Sammael, and that through him there had been revealed the coming of the Beloved from the seventh heaven (Arabot), and his transformation, and his descent, and the form into which he must be transformed, (namely) the form of a man, and the persecution with which he would be persecuted, and the torments with which the children of Israel must torment him, and the coming of the twelve disciples, and the teaching, and that before the Sabbath the must be crucified on a tree, and be crucified with wicked men and that he would be buried in a grave, and the twelve who (were) with him would be offended at him; and the guards who would guard the grave; and the descent of the angel of the church which is in the heavens, whom he will summon in the last days; and that the angel of the Holy Spirit and Michael **(Author's Note: Regarding the Mystery of Michael & Yahoshua, The Spirit of Michael was the Spirit that Incarnated Yahoshua's Earthly Body, departing after His Crucifixion, He now returns to take that body up, read on...),** the chief of the holy angels, will open his grave on the third day, and that Beloved, sitting on their shoulders, will come forth and send out his twelve disciples, And they will teach all nations and every tongue the resurrection of the Beloved, and those who believe in his crucifixion will be saved, and in his ascension to the seventh heaven (Arabot) from where he came; And that many who believe in him will speak through the Holy Spirit, And there will be many signs and miracles in those days. And afterwards, at his approach, his disciples will abandon the teachings of the twelve apostles, and their faith, and their love, and their purity. And there will be much contention at his coming and at his approach. And in those days (there will be) many who will love office, although lacking wisdom. And there will be many wicked elders and shepherds who wrong their sheep, [and they will be rapacious because they do not have holy shepherds].And many will exchange the glory of the robes of the righteous for the robes of those who love money; and this world. And there will be many slanders and [much] vainglory at the approach of YAHOSHUA, and the Holy Spirit will withdraw from many. And in those days there will not be many prophets, nor those who speak reliable words, except one here and there in different places, because of the spirit of error and of fornication, and of vainglory, and of the love of money, which there will be among those who are said to be servants of that One, and among those who receive that One. And among the shepherds and the elders there will be great hatred towards one another. For there will be great jealousy in the last days, for everyone will speak whatever pleases him in his own eyes. And they will make ineffective the prophecy of the prophets who were before my visions and me also. They will make ineffective, in order that they may speak what bursts out of their heart.

The reign of Beliar

Now, therefore, Hezekiah and Josab my son, [these are the days of the Completion of the world]. And after it has been brought to completion, Beliar will descend, the great angel, the king of this world, who has ruled ever since it existed. He will descend from his firmament in the form of a man, a king of iniquity, a murderer of his mother- this is the king of this world and will persecute the plant which the twelve apostles of the Beloved will have planted; some of the twelve will be given into his hand. This angel, Beliar, will come in the form of that king, and with him will come all the powers (fallen elohim) of this world, and they will obey him in every wish. By his word he will cause the sun to rise by night, and the moon also he will make to appear at the sixth hour. And he will do everything he wishes in the world; he will act and speak like the Beloved, and will say, *"I am The Messiah, and before me there was no one."* And all men in the world will believe in him. They will sacrifice to him and will serve him, saying, *"This is the Messiah and besides him there is no other."* And the majority of those who have associated together to receive the Beloved he will turn aside after him. And the power of his miracles will be in every city and he will rule for three years and seven months and twenty-seven days. And many faithful and righteous, when they saw him for whom they were hoping, who was crucified, YAHOSHUA THE MESSIAH- after I, Isaiah, had seen him who was crucified and ascended – and who believed in him, of these few will be left in those days as his servants, fleeing from desert to desert as they await his coming. And after [one thousand] three hundred and thirty-two days YAHOSHUA THE MESSIAH will come with his angels and with the hosts of the righteous. From the seventh heaven (Arabot), with the glory of the seventh heaven (Arabot), and Will drag Beliar, and his hosts also, into Gehenna. And he will give rest to the pious whom he finds in the body in this world, but the sun will be ashamed, and (to) all who because of their faith in him have cursed Beliar and his kings. But the righteous will come with YAHOSHUA THE MESSIAH with their robes which are stored up in the seventh heaven (Arabot) above; with YAHOSHUA THE MESSIAH will come those whose spirits are clothed, they will Descend and be present in the world, and YAHWEH will strengthen those who are found in the body, together with the righteous in the Robes of the righteous, and will serve those who have kept watch in this World. And after this they will be turned in their robes upwards, and their body will be left in the world. Then the voice of the Beloved will reprove in anger this heaven, and this earth, and the mountains, and the hills, and the cities, and the desert, and the trees, and the angel of the sun, and that of the moon, and everywhere that Beliar has appeared and acted openly in this world. There will be a resurrection and a judgment in their midst in those days, and the Beloved will cause fire to rise from him, and it will consume all the impious, and they will become as if they had not been created. And the rest of the words of the vision are written in the vision of Babylon. And the rest of the vision about YAHOSHUA THE MESSIAH, behold it is written in the parables in the words of mine that are written in the book which I prophesied openly. And the descent of the Beloved into Sheol, behold it is written in the section where YAHWEH says, *"Behold, my son shall understand."* And all these things, behold they are written in the Psalms, in the parables of David the son of Jesse, and in the Proverbs of Solomon his son, and in the words of Korah and of Ethan the Israelite, and in the words of Asaph, and in the rest of the psalms which the angel of the spirit has inspired,(namely) in those which have no name written, and in the words of Amos my father and of Hosea the prophet, and of Micah, and of Joel and of Nahum, and of Jonah, and of Obadiah, and of Habakkuk, and of Haggai, and of Zephaniah, and of Zechariah, and of Malachi, and in the words of the righteous Joseph, and in the words of Daniel.

The execution of Isaiah
Because of these visions, therefore, Beliar was angry with Isaiah, and he dwelt in the heart of Manasseh, and he sawed Isaiah in half with a wood saw. And while Isaiah was being sawed in half, his accuser. Belkira, stood by, and all the false prophets stood by, laughing and (maliciously) joyful because of Isaiah. And Belkira, through Mekembekus, stood before Isaiah, laughing and deriding. And Belkira said to Isaiah, *"say, I have lied in everything I have spoken; the ways of Manasseh are good and right, and also the ways of Belkira and those who are with him are good."* And he said this to him when he began to

be sawed in half. And Isaiah was in a vision of YAHWEH, but his eyes were open, and he saw them. And Belkira spoke thus to Isaiah, *"say what I say to you, and I will turn their heart and make Manasseh, and the princes of Judah and the people, and all Jerusalem worship you."* And Isaiah answered and said, *"If it is within my power to say, Condemned and cursed be you, and all your hosts, and all your house! for there is nothing further that you can take except the skin of my body."* And they seized Isaiah the son of Amoz and sawed him in half with a wood saw. And Manasseh, and Belkira, and the false prophets, and the princes, and the people and all stood by looking on. And to the prophets who (were) with him he said before he was sawed in half, *"Go to the district of Tyre and Sidon, because for me alone YAHWEH has mixed the cup."* And while Isaiah was being sawed in half, he did not cry out , or weep, but his mouth spoke with the Holy Spirit until he was sawed in two. Beliar did this to Isaiah through Belkira and through Manasseh, for Sammael was very angry with Isaiah from the days of Hezekiah, king of Judah, because of the destruction of Sammael which he had seen through YAHWEH, while Hezekiah his father was king. And he did as Satan wished.

Isaiah visits Hezekiah and has a vision
In the twentieth year of the reign of Hezekiah, king of Judah, Isaiah the son of Amoz and Josab the son of Isaiah came to Hezekiah in Jerusalem from Gilgal. And he sat on the couch of the king, and they brought a seat for him, but he would not sit (on it). And when Isaiah began to speak with Hezekiah the king the words of faith and righteousness, all the princes of Israel were sitting (there), and the eunuchs and the king's counselors. And there were there forty prophets and sons of the prophets who had come from the neighboring districts, and from the Mountains, and from the country, when they had heard that Isaiah was coming from Gilgal to Hezekiah. They came that they might greet him, and that they might hear His words, and that he might lay his hand on them, and that they might prophesy, and that he might hear their prophesy; and they were all in the presence of Isaiah. And when Isaiah spoke with Hezekiah the words of Righteousness and faith, they all heard a door being opened and the voice of the Spirit. And the king summoned all the prophets and all the people Who were to be found there, and they came. And Micah, and the aged Anaias, and Joel and Josab were sitting on his right. And when they all heard the voice of the Holy Spirit, they all Worshiped on their knees, and they praised the ELOHIM of righteousness, the Most High, the One who (dwells) in the upper world and who sits on high, the Holy One, the One who rests among the holy ones, and they ascribed glory to the One who had thus

graciously given a door in an alien world, had graciously given it to a man. And while he was speaking with the Holy Spirit in the hearing of them all, he became silent, and his mind was taken up from him, and he did not see the men who were standing before him. His eyes indeed were open, but his mouth was silent, and the Mind in his body was taken up from him. But his breath was (still) in him, for he was seeing a vision. And the angel who was sent to show him (the vision) was not of this firmament, nor was he from the angels of glory of this world, but he came from the seventh heaven (Arabot) And the people who were standing by, apart from the circle of prophets, did [not] think that the holy Isaiah had been taken up. And the vision which he saw was not from this world, but from the world which is hidden from the flesh. And after Isaiah had seen this vision he recounted it to Hezekiah, and to Josab his son, and to the other prophets who had come. But the officials, and the eunuchs, and the people did not hear, apart from Samnas to secretary, and Jehoiakim, and Asaph the recorder, for they (were) doers of righteousness, and the fragrance of the Spirit was in them; but the people did not hear, for Micah and Josab his son had sent them out when the wisdom of this world was taken from him as if he were dead.

Isaiah's journey through the seven heavens
The vision which Isaiah saw he told to Hezekiah, and to Josab his son, and to Micah, and to the other prophets it was as follows: *"When I prophesied in accordance with the message which you have heard, I saw a glorious angel; his glory was not like the glory of the angels which I always used to see, but he had great glory, and an office, such that I cannot describe the glory of this angel. And I saw when he took hold of me by my hand, and I said to him, 'Who are you? And what is your name? And where are you taking me up?' For strength had been given to me that I might speak with him. And he said to me, "When I have taken you up through (all) The stages and have shown you the vision on account of which I was sent, then you will understand who I am; but my name you will not know, or you have to return into this body. But where I take you up, you will see, because for this purpose I was sent." And I rejoiced because he spoke to me with kindness. And he said to me, "Do you rejoice because I have spoken kindly to you?" And he said, "You will see one greater than me, how he will speak kindly and gently with you; and the Father of the one who is greater you will also see, because for this purpose I was sent from the seventh heaven (Arabot), that I might make all this clear to you."*

The Firmament - And we went up into the firmament, I and he and there I saw Sammael and his hosts; and there was a great struggle in it, and the words of Satan, and they were envying on another. And as above, so also on earth, for the likeness of what (is) in the firmament is here on earth. And I said to the angel, *"What is this envying?"* And he said to me, *"So it has been ever since this world existed until now, and this struggle (will last) until the one comes whom you are to see, and he will destroy him"*

The first heaven (Willon) - And after this he took me up above the firmament; this is the [first] heaven. There I saw a throne in the middle, and on the right and on the left of it there were angels. And [the angels on the left] were not like the angels who stood on the right, but those who stood on the right had more glory, and they all sang praises with one voice. And the throne was in the middle, and it they praised, and those on the left after them; but their voice was not like the voice of those on the right, nor their praise like the praise of those (on the right) And I asked the angel who led me and said to him, *"To whom is this praise directed?"* And he said to me, *"To the praise of [the One who sits in] the seventh heaven (Arabot), the One who rests in the holy world, and to his beloved, from where I was sent to you. To there it is directed."*

The second heaven (Raqia) - And again, he took me up into The second heaven (Raqia), and the height of that heaven is like that from heaven to earth and to the firmament. And [I saw there, as] in the first heaven (Willon), angels on the right and on the left, and a throne in the middle, and the praise of the angels who (were) in The second heaven (Raqia); and the one who sat on the throne in The second heaven (Raqia) had more glory than all (the rest). And there was great glory in The second heaven (Raqia), and their praise was not like the praise of those who (were) in the first heaven (Willon). And I fell on my face to worship him, and the angel who led me would not let me, but said to me, *"Worship neither throne, nor angel from the six heavens, from where I was sent to lead you, before I tell you in the seventh heaven (Arabot). For above all the heavens and their angels is placed your throne, and also your robes and your crown which you are to see. And I rejoiced very much that those who love El Elyon and his Beloved will at their end go up there through the angel of the Holy Spirit."*

The third heaven (Shaqim) - And he took me up into the third heaven (Shaqim), and in the same way I saw those who (were) on the right and on the left, and there also (there was) a throne in the middle and one who sat (on it), but no mention of this world was made there. And I said to the angel who (was) with me, for the glory of my face was being transformed as I went up from heaven to heaven, *"Nothing of the vanity of that world is named here."* And he answered me, saying, *"Nothing is named because of its weakness, but nothing is hidden which is done there."* And I wished to find out how it is known; and he answered me, saying, *"When I have taken you up into the seventh heaven (Arabot), from where I was sent, to the One which (is) above these, then you will know that nothing is hidden from the thrones and those who dwell in the heavens, nor from the angels."* And the praises which they sang and the glory of the One who sat on the throne were great, and the angels who (were) on the right and on the left had more glory than (those in) the heaven which (was) below them.

The fourth heaven (Zebul) - And again he took me up into the fourth heaven (Zebul), and the height from the third to the fourth heaven (Zebul) was greater than (from) earth to the firmament. And there I again saw those who (were) on the right and those who (were) on the left, and the one who sat on the throne was in the middle, and there also they were singing praises. And the praise and glory of the angels on the right was greater than that of those on the left. And again the glory of the one who sat on the throne was greater than that of the angels who (were) on the right, but their glory (was) greater than that of those below.

The fifth heaven (Maon) - And he took me up into the fifth heaven (Maon). And again I saw those who (were) on the right and the left, and the one who sat on the throne had more glory than those of the fourth heaven (Zebul). And the glory of those who (were) on the right was greater than that of those who (were) on the left the glory of the one on the throne was greater than that of the angels who (were) on the right, But their praise was more glorious than that of the fourth heaven (Zebul). And I praised the One who is not named and is unique, who dwells in the heavens, whose name is unknown to all flesh. The One who has given such glory to the different heavens, who makes the glory of the angels great and the glory of the one who sits on the throne (even) greater. The air of the sixth heaven (Makon)

And again, he took me up into the air of the sixth heaven (Makon), and I saw a splendor such as I had not seen in the five heavens as I Went up; the angels possessed great glory, and the praise there was holy and wonderful. And I said to the angel who led me, *"What (is) this which I*

See, my master?" And he said to me, *"I am not your master, but your Companion."* And again I asked him, and I said to him, *"Why (are there) not Corresponding groups of angels?"* And he said to me, *"From the sixth heaven (Makon) and upwards there are no longer those on the left, nor is there a throne placed in the middle, but [they are directed] by the power of the seventh heaven (Arabot), where the One who is not named dwells, and his Chosen One, whose name is unknown, and no heaven can learn his name, for he is alone, (he) whose voice all the heavens and thrones answer. I, therefore, have been empowered and sent to bring you up here that you may see this glory, and (that) you may see YAHWEH of all these heavens and of these thrones being transformed until he resembles your appearance and your likeness. But I say to you, Isaiah, that no man who has to return into a Body of that world [has come up, or seen], or understood what you have seen and what you are to see, for you are destined in the lot of YAHWEH, the lot of the tree, to come here, and from there is the power of the sixth heaven (Makon) and of the air."* And I proclaimed the greatness of YAHWEH with praise, that through his lot I should come here. And he said to me, *"Hear then this also from your companion [when from the body by the will of ELOHIM you have come up here], then you will receive the robe which you will see, and also other numbered robes placed (there) you will see, and then you will be equal to the angels who (are) in the seventh heaven (Arabot)."*

The sixth heaven (Makon) – and he took me up into the sixth heaven (Makon), And there were none on the left, nor a throne in the middle, but all (were) of one appearance, and their praise (was) equal. And (strength) was given to me, and I also sang praises with Them, and that angel also, and our praise was like theirs. And there they all named the primal Father and his Beloved, Messiah, and the Holy Spirit, all with one voice, but it was not like the voice of the angels who (were) in the five heavens, nor (was it) like their speech, but there was a different voice there, and there was much light there. And then, when I was in the sixth heaven (Makon), I thought that light Which I had seen in the five heavens darkness. And I rejoiced and praised the One who has graciously given Such light to those who await his promise. And I entreated the angel who led me that from then on I Should not return to the world of flesh. Indeed I say to you, Hezekiah and Josab, my son, and Micah, That there is much darkness here. And the angel who led me knew what I thought and said to Me, *"If you rejoice over this light, how much more (will you Rejoice) in the seventh heaven (Arabot) when you see the light where YAHWEH is and his Beloved- from where I was sent – who is to be called in the world of the Son! He* *who is to be in the corruptible world has not (yet) been Revealed, nor the robes, nor the thrones, nor the crowns which are placed (there) for the righteous, for those who believe in that YAHWEH who will descend in your form. For the light which (is) there (is) great and wonderful. But as regards your not returning into the body, your days are not yet complete for coming here."* And when I heard (this), I was sad; and he said to me, *"Do Not be sad."*

The air of the seventh heaven (Arabot)
And he led me into the air of the seventh heaven (Arabot), and moreover I heard a voice saying, *"How far is he who dwells among aliens to go up?"* And I was afraid and was trembling. And he said to me when I was trembling, *"Behold!"* From there another voice which was sent out has come, and it says, *'The holy Isaiah is permitted to come up here, for his robe is here.''* And I asked the angel who (was) with me and said, *"Who is the one who prevented me, and who is this one who turned to me that I might go up?"* And he said to me, *"The one who prevented you, this is the One [who (is) in charge of] the praise of the sixth heaven (Makon). And the one who turned to you, this is your Master, the Messiah, who is to be called in the world YAHOSHUA, but you cannot hear his name until you have come up from this body."* And he took me up into the seventh heaven (Arabot), and there I saw a Wonderful light, and also angels without number. And there I saw the holy Abel and all the righteous from the time of Adam onwards. And there I saw Enoch and all who (were) with him, stripped of (their) robes of the flesh; and I saw them in their robes of above, and they were like the angels who stand there in great glory. But they were not sitting on their thrones, nor were their crowns of glory on them. And I asked the angel who (was) with me, "How is it that they have received these robes, but are not on (their) thrones nor in (their) crowns? And he said to me, *"They do not receive the crowns and thrones of glory – nevertheless, they do see and know whose (will be) the thrones and whose the crowns- until the Beloved descends in the form in which you will see him descend. YAHWEH will indeed descend into the world in the last days, (he) who is to be called Messiah after he has descended and become like you in form, and they will think that he is flesh and a man. And the power (fallen elohim) of that world will stretch out [his hand against the Son], and they will lay their hands upon him and hang (by nails) him upon a tree, not knowing who he is. And thus his descent, as you will see, will be concealed even from the heavens so that it will not be known who he is. And when he has plundered the angel of death, he will rise on the third day and will remain in that world for five hundred and forty-five days. And then*

33

many of the righteous will ascend with him, whose spirits do not receive (their) robes until The Messiah ascends and they ascend with him. Then indeed they will receive their robes and their thrones and their crowns, when he has ascended into the seventh heaven (Arabot)."

The record of men's deeds

And I said to him what I had asked him in the third heaven (Shaqim), *["Show me how everything] which is done in that world is known here."* And while I was still speaking to him, behold one of the angels who were standing by, more glorious than that angel who had brought me up from the world, showed me (some) books, but not like the books of this world; and he opened them, and the books had writing in them, but not like the books of this world. And they were given to me, and I read them, and behold the deeds of the children of Israel were written there, their deeds which you know, my so Josab. And I said, *"Truly, nothing which is done in this world is hidden in the seventh heaven (Arabot)."*

The robes and thrones and crowns

And I saw many robes placed there, and many thrones and many crowns. And I said to the angel who led me, *"Whose (are) these robes and thrones and crowns?"* And he said to me, *"As for the robes, there are many from that world who will receive (them) through believing in the words of that one who will be named as I have told you, and they will keep them, and believe in them, and believe in his crucifixion (and ascension) ; [for them (are) these] placed (here)."*

The worship of YAHWEH

And I saw one standing (there) whose glory surpassed that of all, and his glory was great and wonderful. And when they saw him, all the righteous whom I had seen and the angels came to him. And Adam and Abel and Seth and all the righteous approached first and worshipped him, and they all praised him with one voice, and I also was singing praises with them, and my praise was like theirs. And then all the angels approached, and worshipped, and sang praises. And he was transformed and became like an angel. And then the angel who led me said to me, *"Worship this one,"* and I worshiped and sang praises. And the angel said to me, *"This is YAHWEH of all the praise which you have seen."*

The worship of the Holy Spirit

And while I was still speaking, I saw another glorious (person) who was like him, and the righteous approached him, and worshiped, and sang praises, and I also sang praises with them; but his glory was not transformed to accord with their form. And then the angels approached and worshiped him. And I saw YAHWEH and the second angel, and they were standing, and the second one whom I saw (was) on the left of YAHWEH. And I asked the angel who led me and I said to him, "Who is this one?" And he said to me, *"Worship him, for this is the angel of the Holy Spirit who has spoken in you and also in the other righteous."*

The worship of ELOHIM

And I saw the Great Glory while the eyes of my spirit were open, but I could not thereafter see, nor the angel who (was) with me, nor any of the angels whom I had seen worship YAHWEH. But I saw the righteous as they beheld with great power the Glory of that One. And my Master approached me, and the angel of the Spirit, and said, *"See how it has been given to you to see YAHWEH, and (how) because of you power has been given to the angel who (is) with you."* And I saw how my Master and the angel of the Holy Spirit worshiped and both together praised YAHWEH. And then all the righteous approached and worshiped, and the angels approached and worshiped, and all the angels sang praises. The worship of the Father by the six lower heavens

And then I heard the voices and the hymns of praise which I had heard in each of the six heavens- which I had heard as I ascended there; and all (the voices and hymns of praise) were directed to that Glorious One whose glory I could not see. And I also heard and saw the praise (which was directed to) him, and YAHWEH and the angel of the Spirit heard everything. And all the praise which was sent (up) from the six heavens was not only heard, but seen. And I heard the angel who led me, and he said to me, "This is El Elyon of the high ones, who dwells in the holy world, who rests among the holy ones, who will be called by the Holy Spirit in the mouth of the righteous the Father of YAHOSHUA."

YAHOSHUA is commissioned by the Father

And I heard the voice of El Elyon, the Father, as he said to My Master, Ha Mashiach (the Anointed One), who will be called YAHOSHUA, *"Go out and descend through all the heavens. You shall descend through the firmament and through that world as far as the angel who (is) in Sheol, but you shall not go as far as Perdition. And you shall make your likeness like that of all who (are) in the five heavens, and you shall take care to make your form like that of the angels of the firmament and also (like that) of the angels who (are) in*

*Sheol. And none of the angels of that world shall know that you (are)
Master with me of the seven heavens and of their angels. And they
shall not know that you (are) with me when with the voice of the
heavens I summon you, and their angels and their lights, and when I
lift (my voice) to the sixth heaven (Makon), that you may judge and
destroy the princes and the angels and the powers (fallen elohim) of
that world, and the world which is ruled by them, for they have denied
me and said, 'We alone are, and there is no one besides us.' And
afterwards you shall ascend from the powers (fallen elohim) of death
to your place, and you shall not be transformed in each of the
heavens, but in glory you shall ascend and sit at my right hand, and
then the princes and the powers of that world will worship you."* This
command I heard the Great Glory giving to my Master.

The Descent of YAHOSHUA through the seven heavens
And thus I saw when my Master went out from the seventh heaven
(Arabot) into the sixth heaven (Makon). And the angel who had led
me from this world was with me, and he said to me, *"Understand,
Isaiah, and look, that you may see the transformation and descent of
YAHOSHUA."* And I looked, and when the angels who (were) in the
sixth heaven (Makon) saw him, they praised him and glorified him,
for he had not been transformed into the form of the angels there; and
they praised him, and I also sang praises with them. And I saw when
he descended into the fifth heaven (Maon), that in the fifth heaven
(Maon) he made his form like that of the angels there, and they did not
praise him, for his form was like theirs. And then he descended into
the fourth heaven (Zebul) and made his form like that of the angels
there; and when they saw him, they did not praise him or glorify him,
for his form (was) like their form. And again I saw when he
descended into the third heaven (Shaqim), that he made his form like
that of the angels who (were) in the third heaven (Shaqim). And those
who kept the gate of the (third) heaven demanded the password, and
YAHOSHUA gave (it) to them in order that he should not be
recognized; and when they saw him, they did not praise him or glorify
him, for his form (was) like their form. And again I saw when he
descended into The second heaven (Raqia), that there again he gave
the password, for those who kept the gates demanded (it), and the
master gave (it). And I saw when he made his form like that of the
angels who (were) in The second heaven (Raqia), that they saw him,
but did not praise him, for his form (was) like their form. And again I
saw when he descended into the first heaven the first heaven (Willon),
that there he gave the password to those who kept the gates. And he
made his form like that of the angels who (were) on the left of that

throne, and they did not praise him or glorify him, for his form (was) like their form. And as for me, no one questioned me because of the angel who led me. And Again he descended into the firmament where the prince of this world dwells, and he gave the password to those who (were) on the left, and his form (was) like theirs, and they did not praise him there; but in envy they were fighting one another, for there is there a power of evil and envying about trifles. And I saw when he descended and made himself like the angels of the air, that he was like one of them. And he did not give the password, for they were plundering and doing violence to one another.

The miraculous birth of YAHOSHUA

And after this I looked, and the angel who spoke to me and led me said to me, *"Understand, Isaiah son of Amoz, because for this purpose I was sent from YAHWEH."* And I saw a woman of the family of David the prophet whose name (was) Mary, and she (was) a virgin and was betrothed to a man whose name (was) Joseph, a carpenter, and he also (was) of the seed and family of the righteous David of Bethlehem in Judah. And he came into his lot. And when she was betrothed, she was found to be pregnant, and Joseph the carpenter wished to divorce her. But the angel of the Spirit appeared in this world, and after This Joseph did not divorce Mary; but he did not reveal this matter to anyone. And he did not approach Mary, but kept her as a holy virgin, although she was pregnant. And he did not live with her for (another) two months (after this discovery that she was pregnant). And after two months of days, while Joseph and Mary his wife were alone....., It came about that Mary then looked with her eyes and saw a small infant, and she was astounded. And after her astonishment had worn off, her womb was found as (it was) at first, before she had conceived. And when her husband, Joseph, said to her, *"what has made you astounded?"* his eyes were opened, and he saw the infant and praised YAHWEH, because YAHOSHUA the Messiah had come in his lot. And a voice came to them, *"Do not tell this vision to anyone."* But the story about the infant was spread abroad in Bethlehem. Some said, *"The virgin Mary has given birth before she has been married two months."* But many said, *"She did not give birth; the midwife did not go up (to her), and we did not hear (any) cries of pain."* And they were all blinded concerning him; they all knew about him, but they did not know from where he was. And they took him and went to Narazeth in Galilee. And I saw, O Hezekiah and Josab my son, and say to the other prophets also who are standing by, that it was hidden from all the heavens and all the princes and every elohim of this world.

The infancy and life of YAHOSHUA THE MESSIAH
And I saw (that) in Nazareth he sucked the breast like an infant, as was customary, that he might not be recognized. And when he had grown up, he performed great signs and miracles in the land of Israel and (in) Jerusalem.

The crucifixion and resurrection of YAHOSHUA the Messiah
And after this the adversary envied him and roused the children of Israel, who did not know who he was, against him. And they handed him to the ruler, and crucified him, and he descended to the angel who (is) in Sheol. In Jerusalem, indeed, I saw how they crucified him on a tree, And likewise (how) after the third day he rose and remained (many) days.

The ascension of YAHOSHUA through the seven heavens
And the angel who led me said to me, *"Understand, Isaiah."* And I saw when he sent out the twelve disciples and ascended. And I saw him, and he was in the firmament, but was not transformed into their form. And all the angels of the firmament, and Satan, saw him and worshiped. And there was much sorrow there as they said, *"How did YAHOSHUA THE MESSIAH descend upon us, and we did not notice the glory which was upon him, which we (now) see was upon him from the sixth heaven (Makon)?"* And he ascended into The second heaven (Raqia), and he was not transformed, but all the angels who (were) on the right and on the left, and the throne in the middle, worshiped him, and praised him, and said, *"How did YAHOSHUA THE MESSIAH remain hidden from us as he descended, and we did not notice?"* And in the same way he ascended into the third heaven (Shaqim), and in the same way they praised him and spoke. And in the forth heaven and also in the fifth they spoke in exactly the same way. But there was one glory, and from it he was not transformed. And I saw when he ascended into the sixth heaven (Makon), that they worshiped him and praised him; but in all the heavens the praise grew louder. And is saw how he ascended into the seventh heaven (Arabot), and all the righteous and all the angels praised him. And then I saw that he, sat down at the right hand of that Great Glory, whose glory I told you I could not behold. And also I saw that the angel of the Holy Spirit sat on the left.

The conclusion of the vision – This angel said to me, *"Isaiah, son of Amoz, [it is enough for you], for these (are) great things, for you have observed what no one born of flesh has observed. And you shall return*

into your robe until your days are complete; then you shall come here."
These things I saw.

Isaiah's instructions to Hezekiah – And Isaiah told (them) to all those who were standing before him, and they sang praises. And he spoke to Hezekiah the king and said, *"These things I have spoken. And the end of this world and all this vision will be brought about in the last generation."* And Isaiah made him swear that he would not tell this to the people of Israel, and that he would not allow any man to copy these words. And then they shall read them. But as for you, be in the Holy Spirit that you may receive your robes, and the thrones and the crowns of glory, which are placed in the seventh heaven (Arabot). Because of these visions and prophecies Sammael Satan sawed Isaiah the son of Amoz, the prophet, in half by the hand of Manasseh. And Hezekiah gave all these things to Manasseh in the twenty-sixth year of his reign. But Manasseh did not remember these things, nor place them in his heart, but became the servant of Satan and was destroyed. Here ends (the book) of Isaiah the prophet with his ascension.

THE LUCIFERIC REBELLION

Lucifer was a brilliant son of the celestial beings of the local universe of Nebadon called Lanonondek. He had experience serving in many systems and had been a high counselor of his order - distinguished for wisdom, sagacity, and efficiency and was designated as one of the hundred most able and brilliant beings in more than seven hundred thousand of his order.

From such a magnificent beginning, through evil and error, he embraced sin and now is numbered as one of three system Rulers in the local universe Nebadon who has succumbed to the desire of personal liberty over universal allegiance and the obligation of brotherhood.

In the Local Universe, the domain of Michael (Yahoshua the Messiah), there are ten thousand systems of inhabited worlds. Throughout these thousands of systems and the universe headquarters, only three Systems Rulers have ever been found in contempt of the government of the Creator Son, Michael (Yahoshua the Messiah).

War in Heaven and The Leaders

of Rebellion

Lucifer – like mortals - was not an 'ascending being;' (a being created to grow to a higher state of existence) he was a Created Son of the local universe, and of him it was said: *"You were perfect in all your ways from the day you were created till unrighteousness was found in you."* Ezekiel 28:14-17

Many times had he been in counsel with the Supreme Beings of Edentia on the mansion worlds. And Lucifer reigned *"upon the holy mountain of Elohim,"* the administrative mount Yahrusem, which is also one of the mansion worlds in the local universe, for he was the chief executive of a great system of 607 inhabited worlds.

Lucifer was a magnificent being, a brilliant character; he stood next to the elohim of the constellations in the direct line of universe authority. Notwithstanding Lucifer's transgression, subordinate intelligence refrained from showing him disrespect and disdain prior to Michael's bestowal on Earth as Yahoshua the Messiah.

Even the archangel of Michael, at the time of Moses' resurrection, *"did not bring against him an accusing judgment but simply said, 'the judge rebuke you."* Jude1:9 Judgment in such matters belongs to the Ancients of Days, the rulers of the superuniverse.

Lucifer is now the fallen and deposed Ruler of the mansion world called Satania. Arrogance is most disastrous, and regarding Lucifer it was said: *"Your heart was lifted up because of your beauty; you corrupted your wisdom because of your brightness."* The prophet Isaiah saw his sad estate when he wrote: *"How are you fallen from heaven, O Lucifer, son of the morning! How are you cast down, you who dared to confuse the nations of the world!"* Is. 14:12-22

Be it known that Lucifer has children on this earth that are ruling the earth temporarily now and have established a new world order called the Illuminati, which is causing great iniquity throughout all the earth. Very little was known of or heard of Lucifer on Earth because he assigned his first lieutenant, Satan, to advocate his cause on Earth. Satan was a member of the same primary celestial group as Lucifer but never functioned as a System Ruler (or Sovereign). Satan entered fully into the Lucifer rebellion. The "Devil" is none other than Caligastia, the deposed planetary prince of the Earth and son of the secondary celestial order the same order as Lucifer and Satan. At the time Michael was on the Earth as Yahoshua the Messiah, in the flesh, Lucifer, Satan, and the Devil Caligastia were leagued together to effect the miscarriage of Michael (Yahoshua the Messiah) of his bestowal mission on earth.

To better understand this think of the movie Star Wars, for this is the true account of Star Wars and the dark Lords. *And there was War in Heaven: Michael and his angels fought against the dragon; and the dragon fought and his angels, and prevailed not; neither was their place found anymore in heaven. And the great dragon was cast out, that old serpent, called the devil, and Satan, which deceiveth the whole world; he was cast out into the earth, and his angels were cast out with him.* Rev. 12:8-10 But they Lucifer, Satan and the devil Caligastia signally failed.

Abadon was the chief of the staff of the devil Caligastia. He followed his master into rebellion and has ever since acted as chief executive of the Earth's rebels, who has been imprisoned in the bottomless pit for a season by Yahoshua the Messiah (Rev. 1:12). Beelzebub was the leader of the disloyal Midway Creatures who allied themselves with the forces of the traitorous devil Caligastia.

The dragon eventually becomes the symbolic representation of all these evil personages.

Dragon is Tanin (תנן), one who devours, howls and laments

Upon the triumph of Michael (Yahoshua the Messiah), *"Gabriel came down from Salvington of our Local Universe and bound the dragon (all the rebel leaders) for an age."* Lucifer's children are still on earth and have sworn allegiance to their Father under the new world order the illuminati, and is acting on the behalf of their imprisoned father who behaves like a dragon. Of the seraphic rebels of Yahrusem it is written: *"And the angels who kept not their first estate but left their own habitation, he has reserved in sure chains of darkness to the judgment of the great day."* Jude 1:6

The Cause of Rebellion

The cause of rebellion was caused by the denial of the existence of YAHWEH, the Universal Father, and his Holy Name. Lucifer and his first assistant, Satan, had reigned on the mansion world of Yahrusem in the local universe for more than five hundred thousand years when they began to conceive the rebellion. There were no peculiar or special conditions in the system of Satania that suggested or favored rebellion. The idea took form in Lucifer's mind and he then announced his plans to Satan, though it took several months to corrupt the mind of his able and brilliant associate. However, once Satan converted to the rebel theories, he became a bold and earnest advocate of "self assertion and liberty." (This same *'Spirit of Liberty'* is what is destroying the world today, i.e. the feeling that every human being can do anything he wants to do even if it means breaking the universal laws and commandments of Yahweh El Elyon).

Lucifer became increasingly critical of the entire plan of universe administration but always professed wholehearted loyalty to the supreme rulers. His first outspoken disloyalty was manifested in the occasion of a visit of Gabriel to the mansion world Yahrusem just a few days before the open proclamation of the Lucifer Declaration of Liberty.

The Reality of the Universal Father

Lucifer charged that the Universal Father and his name Yahweh El Elyon did not really exist, that physical gravity and space-energy were inherent in the universe, as so many scientists say today, and that the Father Yahweh El Elyon was a myth invented by the Paradise Sons to enable them to maintain the rule of the universes in the Father's name, Yahweh El Elyon. Lucifer denied that character was a gift of the Universal Father and even suggested that the finaliters were in collusion with the Paradise Sons to foster fraud upon all creation since they never brought back a very clear cut idea of the Universal Father's actual character as it is discernible on Paradise. Lucifer traded on reverence as ignorance. The charge was sweeping, terrible, and blasphemous, which caused a third of the Local Universe of Nebadon to go astray into darkness.

In the universe government of the creator son – Michael (Yahoshua the Messiah), Lucifer contended that the local systems should be autonomous.

Lucifer protested against the right of Michael (Yahoshua the Messiah), the Creator Son, to assume rulership of Nebadon the local universe in the Holy Name of a hypothetical Paradise Father by the Name of Yahweh El Elyon, who required all beings to acknowledge allegiance to Him, an unseen Father. Lucifer asserted that the whole plan of worship was a clever scheme to aggrandize the Paradise Sons. The Lucifer manifesto was issued at the annual conclave on the mansion world Satania on the sea of glass, in the presence of the assembled host (Tzebaoth) of Yahrusem in the local universe on the last day of the year, about two hundred thousand years ago, Earth time. Satan proclaimed that worship could be accorded the universal forces physical, intellectual, and spiritual but that allegiance could be acknowledged only to the actual and present ruler, Lucifer, *'the friend of men and angels'* and the *'Elohim of Liberty.'* He promised the planetary princes that they would rule the worlds as supreme executives. This caused the universe to go into rebellion to this day, and caused false Elohim to exalt themselves to be rulers and worshiped by the worlds - false religions on Earth.

The Sons of Melchizedek were sent to Earth to bring true worship to mankind of the existing Universal Father, El Elyon.

The Holy name of the Universal Father, Yahweh, in the beginning of the Earth age of mankind, was blotted out of the consciousness of mankind for a season. The Earth became Tohu (Formless) and Bohu (empty) Gen. 1:2. This is a type of allegory meaning Lucifer caused the Earth to be formless (Tohu) of the character of the Universal Father, Yahweh El Elyon, and empty (Bohu) of the Holy Spirit dwelling in mankind. The Elohim sent a pair of the loyal sons to the earth, Adam and Hawah (Eve), to replenish the earth with the character and holy spirit of the Universal Father, Yahweh El Elyon. Adam Qudamon was instructed to teach his children to acknowledge the existing and Holy Name of the Father Yahweh El Elyon. The Serpent (Nahash) attacked Adam and Hawah (eve) in every direction that he had power to do (see key terms on serpent or Nahash). Remember Satan is a master deceiver, he was a liar and a murderer from the beginning and a lie and murder he will do. John 8:44

However, Adam was knowledgeable of the Holy Name of Yahweh, and he taught it to his son Seth and Seth to his son Enosh. In the days of Enosh the sons of Adam began to call on the name Yahweh (Gen. 4:26). Nevertheless, Satan continued his deceiving efforts to

45

destroy the thoughts of the Universal Father and his name, Yahweh, in the hearts and minds of mankind. He increased his attack by introducing the names of other Elohim to mankind to distract them from the use and belief of the Universal Father, Yahweh El Elyon.

Satan through his spirit and his children continues the same work today, constantly denying the Holy Name of Yahweh. He makes comments such as: the name of Yahweh did not exist in the beginning or that Yahweh is a local deity of the desert people. In the time of the Kings of Israel, for instance, the ancient Syrians believed and thought the same thing.

> *"And there came a man of Elohim, and spake unto the King of Israel, and said, thus saith Yahweh, because the Syrians have said Yahweh is Elohim of the hills, but he is not Elohim of the Valleys, therefore will I deliver all this great multitude into thine hands, and you shall know that I am Yahweh."*
> 1 Kings 20:28

For such are false apostles, deceitful workers, transforming themselves into apostles of the Messiah. And no marvel for Satan transformeth himself into an angel of light.

Therefore, it is no great thing if his ministers also be transformed as ministers of Righteousness; whose end shall be according to their works, 2 Cor. 11:13-15 Forever learning but denying the power (El) that created them, having a form of worship but denying the power there of.

All of creation, the universe of universes, was created for his namesake. As today, before Abraham the Holy Name of Yahweh was denied, but Abraham began to call on the Holy Name which was revealed to him by Melchizedek. Gen. 13:4

On the Earth today we have those who deny that the name of the Universal Father is, was and always will be: Yahweh El Elyon.

When Moses received his revelation at the burning bush Elohim spoke to him telling him to go down to Egypt and deliver his people the Israelites. And Moses said unto Elohim, when I come unto the Children of Israel, and say unto them, the Elohim of your Fathers hath sent me unto you. And they shall say to me what is his name? What shall I say unto them? And Elohim said unto Moses, *'Ehiyeh Asher Ahiyeh (I will be what I will be)'* And he said, thus shall thou say unto the Children of Israel, *'I will be hath sent me unto you.'* And Elohim said moreover unto Moses, *'this shall you say unto the Children of Israel, Yahweh, the Elohim of your Fathers, the Elohim of Abraham, Isaac, and Jacob, has sent me unto you. This is my name forever, and this my memorial unto all generations.'* Ex. 3:13-15

All of the Holy prophets called on the Holy Name of Yahweh, and they wrote as they were inspired by the Holy Spirit, they did not just make up a name of any deity.

The prophet Isaiah wrote, *"I am Yahweh: that is my name: and my glory will I not give to another, neither my praises to graven images."* Is. 42:8

Yahoshua the Messiah (Yahweh sends Salvation) was sent to the earth to proclaim His name by power and authority with signs and wonders, and to complete his mission as the seventh bestowal - taking up all authority in the universe and Earth. All the great works performed by Yahoshua the Messiah were done in the Holy Name of Yahweh. Yahoshua said, *"I have glorified thee on the earth; I have finished the work which thou gavest me to do."* John 17: *"I have declared thy name unto men which thou gavest me out of the world: Thine they were, and thou gavest them me; and they have kept thy word."* John 17:6

   "In the beginning was the word, and the word was with Yahweh, and the word was Yahweh. The same was in the beginning with Yahweh. All things were made by him ; and without him was not any thing made that was made. In him was life; and the life was the light of men. He was in the world, and the world was made by him, and the world knew him not." John 1:1-10   To this day the world still doesn't know who he is and looks for some physical man to be the Messiah - setting themselves up for mass deception. Only the sons of light will know and understand who he, Yahoshua the Messiah, really is

   At the end of Michael's bestowal mission on Earth, Satan deceived the high priest of Israel to have Yahoshua crucified, then the Messiah made his final statement to the world, saying 'all power is giving unto me in heaven and in earth' gaining the right to be called King of Kings and Ruler or Rulers. On Yahoshua the Messiah's second return to the earth, he will return in his heavenly body and in a glorious form and not in the form of animal flesh. So no man can stand up in spirit and truth and proclaim that he is the Messiah.

   In the world today as it is written – we, the sons of Yahweh, are hated for his name sake, and we look for the day when Yahweh proves Himself to be King over all the earth: "And in that day 'Yahweh will prove to be a unity, and with one name.' Zac. 14:9

THE PLANET EARTH REBELLION

On Earth it is impossible to understand without knowledge of certain great events of the past the occurrence and consequences of the planet Earth rebellion. This upheaval interfered and effected the development of social progress and spiritual development, which has and is profoundly influencing devastating calamities.

Caligastia: The Planetary Prince Betrayal

For three hundred thousand years Caligastia was the planetary prince in charge of the Earth when Satan, Lucifer's assistant, made one of his periodic inspection calls. When Satan arrived on the Earth, his appearance in no way resembled human beings of the earth's caricatures of his nefarious majesty.

He was, and still is a Lanondek Son of great brilliance. And no marvel, for Satan himself is a brilliant creature of light. 2 Cor. 11:13-15

In the course of this inspection, Satan informed Caligastia of Lucifer's then proposed *"Declaration of Liberty"* and the earth's prince, Caligastia, agreed to betray the planet Earth upon the announcement of the rebellion. The loyal universe beings looked with great disdain upon prince Caligastia because of this premeditated betrayal. This announcement of Liberty has caused the earth to be in rebellion from Yahweh El Elyon's commandments up to now. Yahweh El Elyon's only Begotten Son, Michael (Yahoshua the Messiah), voiced this contempt when he said: *"you are like your leader, Lucifer, and you have sinfully perpetuated his iniquity. He was a falsifier and a*

49

deceiver from the beginning of his self exaltation because he abode not in the truth."

There are many ways of looking at sin, but from the universal viewpoint sin is the attitude of a character who is knowingly resisting and breaking universal and cosmic commandments and laws and reality, *"for sin is the breaking of the law"* Rom. 7:7-14 *Error* is a misconception or distortion of Yahweh El Elyon commandment, law or words and reality. *Evil* is a partial realization of, or maladjustment to universal commandment, laws or reality. But sin is a purposeful resistance and breaking of divine laws and commandments or divine reality – a conscious choosing to oppose spiritual progress – while *iniquity* consists in an open and persisted defiance of recognized reality of universal laws and commandments, and signifies to such a degree of character disintegration as to become cosmically insane. Error suggests lack of intellectual keenness; evil, deficiency of wisdom; sin, manifest spiritual poverty; but iniquity indicates a vanishing control of character.

And when sin has so many times been chosen and so often repeated, it often becomes habitual. Habitual sinners usually become iniquitous, wholehearted rebels against the commandments, laws and universal realities. (However, if one repents, all manner of sin may be forgiven except for suicide and blasphemy of the Holy Spirit.)

I doubt whether the established son of iniquity would ever sincerely experience sorrow for his misdeed or accept repentance and forgiveness for his sins.

Caligastia held a prolonged conference with his associate, Daligastia, after which he later called the council of ten of the Earth in an extraordinary session.

The assembly was open with the statement that prince Caligastia (who became The Devil) was about to proclaim himself absolute ruler of Earth and demanded that all administrative groups abdicate by resigning all of their functions and power into the hands of Daligastia as trustee, pending the reorganization of the Earth's government and the redistribution of these offices of administrative authority.

This act and demand of Caligastia took on the action of planetary rebellion. This same counsel of ten is none other than the ten toed nations and kings that will have power with Satan for one hour. Dan. 7:24 Rev.17:12

Because of the rebellion of Caligastia and Dalagastia the whole system of the Earth's circuits had been served; Earth was isolated, it became Bohu and Tohu formless and void of character and spirit adjustment of Yahweh El Elyon.

Every order and group of Celestial life on Earth found itself suddenly and without warning isolated, utterly cut off from outside counsel and advise.

Daligastia formally proclaimed Caligastia "El (Power) of the Earth and supreme overall." This proclamation lead to the fate of every superhuman character on the earth. Seraphim and Cherubim and other celestial beings were involved in the decision of this bitter struggle, this long and sinful conflict.

Many superhuman groups that chanced to be on earth at that time of its isolation were detained here and, like the seraphim and their associates, were compelled to chose between sin and righteousness between the ways of Lucifer and the will of the unseen Father of the Universes Yahweh El Elyon this action of choosing between the Universal Father, Yahweh El Elyon, and Lucifer, righteousness and sin, in the last days mankind will be forced to choose one again once and for all, what will you choose

The traitorous and rebellious prince Caligastia marshaled the disloyal midway creatures and other groups of rebel superhuman beings and organized them to execute his bidding.

There were sixty members of the Earth's planetary staff who went into rebellion and chose Nod as their leader. They worked wholehearted for the rebel prince but soon discovered that they were deprived of the sustenance of the system life circuits.

They awakened to the fact that they had been degraded to the status of mortal beings. They were indeed superhuman but, at the same time, material and mortal. In an effort to increase their numbers, Daligastia ordered immediate resort to sexual reproduction, knowing full well that the original sixty and their forty-four modified Andonite associates were doomed to suffer extinction by death, sooner or later. After the fall of Dalamatia the disloyal staff migrated to the north and east, in and around the landmass we call India today. Their descendants were long known as the Nodites, and their dwelling place as "the land of Nod." Gen. 4:16.

The presence of these supermen and superwomen, stranded by rebellion and mating sexually with the sons and daughters of earth brought about superhuman beings call Nephilim. Gen. 6:4-5

The rebel staff, deprived of spiritual sustenance, eventually died a natural death. And much of the subsequent idolatry and falsity called religion of the human race grew out of the desire to perpetuate the memory of these highly honored beings of the days of Caligastia. The world today has been deceived a third time in its religious views of misunderstanding, lies and deceit by religion. Be it known that the Universal Father and Creator gave no religion to mankind. He established the universe in a righteous order, and that universal spiritual order on earth was and is called and all ways will be called The Universal Spiritual Order of Melchizedek (the way of, teachings, direction, order of righteousness). Amen. In the last days, great war and upheaval will take place on the planet earth, a third of mankind will be destroyed. The sons of darkness are walking the earth today as demons in the flesh, and they are bent on destroying all of mankind especially the sons of light, the stage of destruction is being set in the earth today. Those who will be left will be the sons of light sons of Yahweh El Elyon, for Yahweh knows how to save his own they will be granted everlasting life. The tree of life will be renewed on earth, *"And he showed me a pure river of water of life, clear as crystal, proceeding out of the throne of Yahweh and of the Lamb. In the midst of the street of it, and on either side of the river, was there the tree of life, which bare twelve manner of fruits, and yielded here fruit every month: and the leaves of the tree were for the healing of the nations. And there shall be no more curse: but the throne of Yahweh and of the Lamb shall be in it; and his Servants shall serve him: And they shall see his face; and His Name shall be in their forehead (mind)."* Rev. 22:1-4

1 Enoch (Chapters 45 – 46)

The Lot of the unbelievers:

The New Heaven and New Earth
This is the second parable concerning those who deny the name of YAHWEH and the congregation of the holy ones. Neither will they ascend into heaven, nor will they reach the ground; such will be the lot of the sinners, who will deny the name of the ELOHIM of the spirits, those who in this manner will be preserved for the day of burden and

tribulation. On that day, my Elect One shall sit on the seat of glory and make a selection of their deeds, their resting places will be without number, their souls shall be firm within them when they see my Elect One, those who have appealed to my glorious name. On that day, I shall cause my Elect One to dwell among them, I shall transform heaven and make it a blessing of light forever. I shall (also) transform the earth and make it a blessing, and cause my Elect One to dwell in her. Then those who have committed sin and crime shall not set foot in her. For in peace I have looked (with favor) upon my righteous ones and given them mercy, and have caused them to dwell before me. But sinners have come before me so that by judgment I shall destroy them from before the face of the earth.

At that place, I saw the One to whom belongs the time before time. And his head was white like wool, and there was with him another individual, whose face was like that of a human being. His countenance was full of grace like that of one among the holy angels. And I asked the one – from among the angels – who was going with me, and who had revealed to me all the secrets regarding the One who was born of human beings, who is this, and from whence is he who is going as the prototype of the Before Time? And he answered me and said to me, *"This is the Son of Man, to whom belongs righteousness, and with whom righteousness dwells. And he will open all the hidden storerooms; for the ELOHIM of the spirits has chosen him, and he is destined to be victorious before YAHWEH in eternal uprightness. This Son of Man whom you have seen is the One who would remove the kings and the mighty ones from their comfortable seats and the strong ones from their thrones. He shall loosen the reins of the strong and crush the teeth of the sinners. He shall depose the kings from their thrones and kingdoms. For they do not extol and glorify him, and neither do they obey him, the source of their kingship. The faces of the strong will be slapped and be filled with shame and gloom. Their dwelling places and their beds will be worms. They shall have no hope to rise from their beds, for they do not extol the name of YAWEH. And they have become the judges of the stars of heaven; the raise their hands (to reach) El Elyon while walking upon the earth and dwelling in her. They manifest all their deeds in oppression; all their deeds are oppression. Their power (depends) upon their wealth. And their devotion is to the idols which they have fashioned with their own hands. But they deny the name of YAHWEH. Yet they like to congregate in his houses and (with) the faithful ones who cling to YAHWEH."*

Baruch 4.8-9

Jeremiah Testifies of Yahoshua the ιν.

But the day came in which Yahweh led the people out of Baʋ,. And Yahweh said to Jeremiah, *"Get up, you and the people, and come to the Jordan; and you will say to the people, 'let him who desires Yahweh leave the works of Babylon behind.' And (of) the men who took wives from them, and the women who took husbands from them, let those who hear you cross over, and take them up to Jerusalem; but as for those who do not hear you, you must not lead them there."* And Jeremiah spoke these words to the people, and they got up and came to the Jordan to cross over. And when he told them the words which Yahweh had spoken to him, half of those who had intermarried with them did not want to hear Jeremiah, but said to him, *"we will not leave our wives behind forever, but we will bring them with us back to our city.'* So they crossed over the Jordan and came to Jerusalem. *And Jeremiah stood firm with Baruch and Abimelech saying, 'no man who cohabits with Babylonians will enter this city!'"* and they said among themselves, 'let's get up and return to Babylon, to our place.' And they departed. But when they came to Babylon, the Babylonians came out to meet them saying, *'you will not come into our city, because you hated us and went out from us in secret; for this you will not come in with us. For we made one another swear an oath in the name of our elohim to receive neither you nor your children, since you went out from us in secret.'* And when they learned this, they turned back and came to a desert place some distance from Jerusalem, and they built themselves a city and named it Samaria. And Jeremiah sent to them saying, *'repent, for an angel of righteousness is coming, and he will lead you to your exalted place.'*

And those who were with Jeremiah continued for nine days, rejoicing and offering up sacrifices for the people. But on the tenth day Jeremiah alone offered up a sacrifice. And he prayed a prayer, saying, *'holy holy, holy, incense of the living trees, true light that enlightens me until I am taken up to you; for your mercy I plead, for the sweet voice of the two seraphim I plead, for another fragrant odor of incense. **And may Michael, the archangel of righteousness who opens the gates for the righteous, be the object of my attention until he leads the righteous in.** I implore you, Almighty Yahweh of all Creation, unbegotten and incomprehensible, in whom all judgment was hidden before these things existed."* And as Jeremiah said these things, while standing at the altar with Baruch and Abimelech, he became as one of those who have given up their soul. And Baruch and Abimelech remained weeping and crying in a loud voice, *"woe to us, because our father Jeremiah has left us; the priest of Elohim has departed."* And all the people heard their weeping, and they all ran to them and saw Jeremiah lying on the ground as though dead. And they tore their garments and put dust on their heads and wept bitterly. And after these things, they prepared themselves to bury him. And behold, there came a voice saying, *'do not bury one still living, for his soul is coming into his body again.'* And because they heard the voice, they did not bury him but remained in a circle around his tabernacle for three days, saying, *'at what hour is he going to rise? And after these three days, his soul came into his body and he lifted up his voice in the midst of them all and said, glorify Elohim with one voice! All of you glorify Elohim, and the son of Elohim who awakens us, Yahoshua the light of all the eons, the inextinguishable lamp, the life of faith! And after these times, there will be another four hundred and seventy seven years, and then he is coming to the earth. And the tree of life which is planted in the middle of Paradise will cause all the uncultivated trees to bear fruit, and they will grow and sprout.'* And the trees that had already sprouted and boasted and said, *'we raised our top to the air, 'he will cause them to wither together with the loftiness of their branches. And the firmly rooted tree will cause them to be judged! And what is scarlet will become as white as wool; the snow will be made black; the sweet waters will become salty, and the salty sweet in the great light of the joy of Elohim. And he will bless the islands that they may bear fruit at the word of the mouth of his anointed one. For he will come! And he will go out and choose for himself twelve apostles, that they may preach among the nations, he whom I have seen adorned by his father and coming into the world on the mount of olives; and he will fill the hungry souls.'* And as Jeremiah was saying these things about the son of Elohim, that he is coming into the world, the people became angry and said, *"these once again are the words spoken by Isaiah the son of Amos saying, 'I saw Elohim and the son of Elohim. Come therefore, and let us not kill him by that same death, but let's stone him with stones.'* Now, Baruch and Abimelech were extremely grieved because they wanted to hear in full the mysteries that he had seen. But Jeremiah said to them, be quiet and hear in full mysteries that he had see. But Jeremiah said to them, be quiet and do not weep for they will not kill me until I have described to you everything to say to Baruch and Abimelech. Then the stone, by the command of Elohim took on the likeness of Jeremiah and they were stoning the stone thinking it was Jeremiah. But Jeremiah delivered all the mysteries that he had soon so Baruch and they were stoning the stone thinking it was Jeremiah. But

Jeremiah delivered up all the mysteries that he had seen to Baruch and Abimelech, and then he simply stood in the midst of the people, desiring to bring his stewardship to an end. Then the stone cried out saying, 'o stupid children of Israel, why do you stone me, thinking that I am Jeremiah? Behold, Jeremiah stands in your midst!' and when they saw him, they immediately ran at him with many stones, and his stewardship was fulfilled. And Baruch and Abimelech came and buried him, and they took the stone and put it on his tome after inscribing it thus: *this is the stone that was the ally of Jeremiah."*

Etymology of The Name 'Melchizedek'

(מלכיצדק) Melchitsedek

= The King of Righteousness

1. מלך- Melech = a king or ruler

Associated Words:

(למלך) Le-Ma-lech (verb) = to take counsel, consult, consider, determine, take advice

(מלכות) Mal-coot = Kingdom, kinghood, kingship, royalty, monarch, royal dignity, realm, state, empire, the mention of Yahweh in Prayers

2. צדק Tsedek = Justice, righteousness, truth, honesty*

Associated Words:

(צדק) Tsa-dek = to be right, just, correct, righteous, acquitted

(צדק) Tsadak = to be right, just, correct, righteous acquitted

(צדקה) Tsa-dee-kah = Justice, Justness, fairness, right, merit, good deed, true judgment, piety, mercy, charity, alms, victory

MACHIVENTA MELCHIZEDEK

The Melchizedeks are widely known as emergency sons for they engage in an amazing range of activities on the worlds of a real universe.

When any extraordinary problem arises, or when something unusual is to be attempted, it is quite often a Melchizedek who accepts the assignment.

The ability of the Melchizedek Sons to function in emergencies and on widely divergent levels of the universe, even on the physical levels of the universe, even on the physical level of character manifestation, is peculiar to there order.

Only the Life Carriers share to any degree this metamorphic range of character function. The Melchizedek order of universe sonship has been exceedingly active on Earth. A corps of twelve served in conjunction with the Life Carriers. A later corps of twelve became receivers for Earth shortly after the Caligastia secession and continued in authority until the time of Adam and Eve (Hawah). The twelve Melchizedeks returned to the Earth upon the default of Adam and Eve (Hawah), and they continued thereafter as planetary receivers on down to the day when Michael (Yahoshua the Messiah) of Nazareth, as the Son of Man, became the titular planetary prince of the Earth.

The Incarnation of Machiventa Melchizedek

Revealed truth was threatened with extinction during the millennium, which followed the fall of the Adamic mission on Earth. Though making progress intellectually, the human race was slowly losing ground spiritually. About 3000 BC the concept of Yahweh Elohim had grown very hazy in the minds of men.

The twelve Melchizedek receivers knew of Michael's impending bestowal on the Earth barring the name of the Universal Father Yahweh as Yahoshua (Yahweh sends salvation), but they did not know how soon it would occur; therefore they convened is solemn council and petitioned El Elyon of Edentia one of the seven mansion worlds, that some provision be made for maintaining the light of truth on Earth. This plea was dismissed with the mandate that the conduct of affairs on 606 of Satania mansion world is fully in the hands of the Melchizedek Custodians. The receivers then appealed to the Father Melchizedek for help but only received word that they should continue to uphold truth concerning the Universal Father, Yahweh El Elyon, in the manner of their own election until the arrival of the bestowal son, Michael (Yahoshua the Messiah) who would rescue the Earth's titles from forfeiture and uncertainty.

And it was in consequence of having been thrown so completely on their own resources that Machiventa Melchizedek one of the twelve planetary receivers of Earth, volunteered to do that which had been done only six times in all the history of Nebadon the local universe: to personalize on Earth as a temporary man of the earth, to bestow himself as an emergency son of world ministry. Permission was granted for this adventure by the Universal authorities, and the actual incarnation of Machiventa Melchizedek was consummated near what was to become the City of Salem (Yahrushalem), in Palestine.

The entire materialization of this Melchizedek son was completed by the planetary receivers with the co-operation of the Life Carriers, certain of the master physical controllers, and other celestial beings resident on Earth. It was 1,973 years before the birth of Yahoshua the Messiah that Machiventa Melchizedek was bestowed upon the human race of Earth. His coming was unspectacular; human eyes did not witness his materialization.

He was first seen by mortal man on that eventual day when he entered the tent of Amdon, a Chaldean herder of Sumerian extraction. And the proclamation of his mission was embodied in the simple statement which he made to this shepherd, "I am Melchizedek, Priest of El Elyon, (the Most High Power Over All Powers) the one and only Elohim." It is this Melchizedek who introduced himself to the chosen prophet Abraham and paved his way for the future generation through the Tribes of Israel, in which was chosen to be the priest nation of Yahweh El Elyon to the nations. Melchizedek taught that at some future time another son of El Elyon would come in the flesh as he had come, but that would be born of woman; and that is that Yahoshua the Messiah was a priest, "forever after the order (direction, teachings, way, order) of Melchizedek.

And thus did Melchizedek prepare the way and set the monotheistic stage of world tendency for the bestowal of an actual Paradise Son of the one El Elyon, who he so vividly portrayed as the Father of all, and who he represented to Abraham as a Elohim would accept man on the simple terms of personal faith. And Michael (Yahoshua the Messiah), When he appeared on earth, confirmed all that Melchizedek had taught concerning the Paradise Father Yahweh El Elyon.

THE ANCIENT MELCHIZEDEK

Melchizedek was the Prophet King of Righteousness, the first High Priest of the Order of Yahweh El-Elyon, the Most High Power of Powers, in the Pious Age when mankind walked upright. This Melchizedek was born of a divine manifestation, recorded in the book of Enoch, one of the lost prophetic books of the Bible.

Before the flood of Noah, Melchizedek was taken up into Paradise Eden, which resides in Shehaqim, the third heaven (Shaqim). After the flood, he descended back to earth to build the great Jerusalem (Yah-ru-sha-lay-eem in Hebrew), Yahweh's City of Peace, and to bless and teach Abraham, who Yahweh El-Elyon promised that through his seed all nations would be blessed.

The Birth of Melchizedek - Excerpts from the Second Book of Enoch, Old Testament Pseudopigrapha, pages 202-212:

"And Methuselah said to the people, `*Here is Nir, He will be in front of your face from the present day, as the guide of the princes.*' And the people answered Methuselah, `*let it be so for us, and the Word of Elohim, the Almighty Creator, be just as he said to you.*' And while Methuselah was speaking to the people, his spirit was convulsed, and kneeling on his knees, he stretched out his hands to heaven, praying to Elohim, and his spirit went out. And Nir and all the people hurried and constructed a sepulcher for Methuselah and they placed for him incense and reeds and many holy things.

And Nir came with many praises, and the people lifted up Methuselah's body, glorifying Yahweh; they performed the service for him at the sepulcher which they had made for him and they covered him over.

And the people said, `*How blessed is Methuselah in front of the face of Elohim and in front of the face of all the people!*' And from there they assembled, and Nir said to the people, `*Hurry up today, bring sheep and bulls and turtledoves and pigeons, so that we may make a sacrifice in front of the face of Elohim, and rejoice today. And then go away to your houses.*' And the people gave heed to Nir the priest, and they hurried and they brought them and tied them up at the head of the altar. And Nir took the knife of sacrifice and slaughtered them in front of the face of Elohim. And the people made merry before the Creator all day. They glorified Yahweh Elohim, the Savior of Nir.

And from that day there was peace and order over all the earth in the day of Nir for 202 years. . .

And then the people turned away from Elohim, their Almighty Creator, and they began to be envious, one against the other, and went to war against peoples, and race rose up against race and struggled and insulted one another.

Even if the lips were the same, nevertheless, the heart chose different things. For the devil became ruler for the third time. The first before paradise, the second time was in paradise; the third time was after paradise, and continuing right up to the flood. And there arose disputation and great turbulence. And Nir, the priest, heard and was greatly aggrieved. And he said in his heart, `*in truth I have come to understand how the time has arrived and the saying which Elohim said to Methuselah, the father of my father, Lamekh. . . .* '

The wife of Nir, whose name was Sophinim, was sterile, never having at any time given birth to a child by Nir. And when Sophinim was in the time of her old age, and in the day of her death, she conceived in her womb. But Nir, the priest had not slept with her, nor had he touched her, from the day that the Creator had appointed him to conduct the liturgy in front of the people.

(Therefore) when Sophinim became conscious of her pregnancy, she was ashamed and embarrassed, and she hid herself during her days of pregnancy, showing her conception to no one. And when 282 had been completed, and the time of birth approached, Nir called his wife to his house. And when he saw her he said '*What have you done, oh wife? And why have you disgraced me in front of the people? Now depart from me, and go where you began the disgrace of your womb, so that I might not defile my hands on account of you, and sin in front of Elohim.'*

And Sophinim said to Nir, *'Oh, my El, (strong One), Behold, it is the time of my old age, and the day of my death has arrived. I do not understand how my menopause and the barrenness of my womb have been reversed.'*

And Nir did not believe his wife, and for the second time he said, *'depart from me, or else I might assault you and commit a sin in front of Elohim.'*

And it came to pass, when Nir had spoken to his wife, Sophinim, that she fell down at his feet and died. Nir was extremely distressed and he said in his heart, *'Could this have happened because of my word, since by word and thought a person can sin in front of Elohim, the Almighty Creator? Now may Yahweh Chased, Most Merciful One, have mercy upon me! I know in truth that my hand was not upon her. Glory to Elohim, because no one among mankind knows about this deed which Elohim has done.'*

And Nir hurried, and he shut the door of his house, and he went to Noah, his brother, and he reported to him everything that had happened, and Noah hurried with Nir to his house. And there they discussed her pregnancy and death, *'Don't let yourself be sorrowful, Nir, my brother, for Elohim, has covered up this shameful event, that none of the people will know of it. Now, let us go quickly and bury her secretly.'* And they placed Sophinim on the bed, and they wrapped her around with black garments, prepared her for burial and dug the grave in secret.

Suddenly, a child came out of the dead Sophinim and he sat on the bed at her side. When Noah and Nir came in to bury Sophinim, they discovered the child and were terrified with great fear. For the child was fully developed physically, as a three year old, sitting up next to the dead body of his mother and he spoke, blessing Elohim, the Creator. And as Noah and Nir looked at the child, they saw a badge of priesthood on his chest, and it was glorious in appearance.

And Noah and Nir said, *'Behold, Yahweh is renewing the priesthood through our seed.'* And they hurried and washed the child, and dressed him in the garments of a priest and they gave him holy bread and he at it. And they called his name Melchizedek.

Then Noah and Nir lifted up the body of Sophinim and divested her of the black garments, washed her and clothed her in exceptionally bright garments and built a shrine for her. And they buried her publicly.

And Noah said to his brother Nir, *'look after this child in secret until the appointed time, because the people will become treacherous upon all the earth and will turn away from Yahweh, and because of their ignorance will seek to put him to death.'* And then Noah went away to his own place.

And great lawlessness began to become abundant over all the earth in the days of Nir. And Nir began to worry excessively, especially about the child, saying, *'How miserable it is for me, Yahweh El Olam, Everlasting Creator, that in my days lawlessness has become abundant upon the face of the earth. And I realize how near our end is on account of the lawlessness of the people. And now, Yahweh El Roie, what is the vision about this child, what is his destiny, and what will I do for him?'* And Yahweh heard the prayer of Nir and appeared to him in a night vision. He said to him, *'Nir, the great lawlessness which has come on the earth among the multitude I shall not tolerate. And behold, I desire now to send out a great destruction on the earth and everything that stands in it shall perish. But, concerning the child, don't be anxious, for in a short time, I will send my archangel, Michael. And he will take the child and put him in the paradise of Eden, in the paradise where Adam was formerly for seven years, having the heavens open all the time up until he sinned. And the child will not perish along with those who are perishing in this generation, as I have revealed it, so that Melchizedek will be the priest to all holy priests, and I will establish him so that he will be the head of the priests of the future.'* And Nir, rose from his sleep and blessed Elohim, the Almighty Creator, who had appeared to him, saying: *'Blessed be Yahweh, the Elohim of my fathers, who has told me how he has made a great priest in my day in the womb of my wife. Because I had no child in this tribe who might become the great priest, but this is my son and your servant and you are Yahweh Gedolah, the Great One. . . . Therefore, honor him together with your servants and great priests, with Sit, Enos, Rusi, Anilam, Prasidam, and Maleleil, Serokh, Arusan, Aleem, Enoch, Methuselah, and myself, your servant, Nir.*

And behold, Melchizedek will be the head of the thirteen priests who existed before. And afterward, in the last generation, there will be another Melchizedek, the first of 12 priests. And the last will be head of all, a great archpriest, the Word and Power of Yahweh, who will perform miracles, greater and more glorious than all the previous ones. Melchizedek will be priest and king in the placed Akhusan, that is to say, in the center of the earth, where Adam was created, and there will be his final grave. And in connection with the arch priest it is written how he also will be buried there, where the center of the earth is, just as Adam also buried his own son there, Abel, whom his brother, Cain, murdered.

I know that great confusion has come and in confusion this generation will come to an end; and everyone will perish, except that Noah, my brother will be preserved. And afterwards there will be planting from his tribe, and there will be another people, and another Melchizedek, the head of priests reigning over the people and performing liturgy for Elohim, the Almighty Creator.'

And when the child had been forty days in Nir's tent, Elohim, the Almighty Creator, said to Michael, '*Go down to the earth to Nir, the priest, and take my child, Melchizedek, who is with him, and place him in the paradise of Eden for preservation. For the time is approaching and I will pour out all the water onto the earth, and everything that is on the earth will perish.'*

Michael hurried, and he came down when it was night, and Nir was sleeping on his bed. And Michael appeared to him, and said: 'Thus saith Yahweh, *'Nir, Send the child to me that I entrusted to you.'* And Nir, not realizing who was speaking to him, responded in fear, *'The child is not with me, I don't know who you are.'* And he who was speaking to him answered, *'Don't be frightened, Nir! I am Elohim's archangel. Elohim has sent me, and behold, I shall take the child today. I will go with him and I will place him in the paradise, Eden, and there he will be forever.'*

'And when the twelfth generation shall come into being, and there will be one thousand and seventy years, and there will be born in that generation a righteous man. And Elohim will tell him that he should go out to that mountain where stands the ark of Noah your brother. And he will find there another Melchizedek, who has been living there for seven years, hiding himself from the people who sacrifice to idols, so that they may not kill him. He will bring him out, and he will be the first high priest for El-

Elyon and King in the city of Salem in the style of this Melchizedek, the originator of the priests. The years will be completed up to that time three thousands and four hundred and thirty two from the beginning and the creation of Adam. And from that Melchizedek, the priests will be twelve in number until the great Igumen. That is, the leader will bring out everything visible and invisible.'

And Nir understood the first dream and believed it. And having answered Michael, he said, *'Blessed be Elohim, who has glorified you in my eyes this day! Now, bless your servant, Nir, for we approach the end of this world. Take the child, and do to him just as Elohim has commanded you.'* And Michael took the child on the same night on which he had come down; and he took him on his wings and he placed him in paradise Eden. And Nir got up in the morning, went into his tent and did not find the child. And there was great grief in his heart because he had no other son except Melchizedek. And it was then that Nir ended his life.

And after him there was no priest among the people, and great confusion arose on the earth.

And Elohim called Noah to make an ark, `with 300 lakets in length and in width 50 lakets and in height 30. And two stories in the middle, and its door of one laket. And of their lakets 300, but ours also 15 thousand; and so of theirs 50, but of ours 2000 and 500, and so theirs 30 but of ours 900, and of theirs on laket, but of our 50.' And when the ark was completed, Yahweh opened the doors of heaven and poured rain upon the earth for 150 days, and all flesh - except for Noah and his family - were destroyed.

"And Noah was in the year 500, and he fathered three sons, Shem, Ham and Japheth. After 100 years, after the birth of his three sons, he went into the ark in the month of Luars, according to the Hebrews and the month of Famenoth, according to the Egyptians, on the 18th day. And the ark floated for forty days. And in all they were in the ark for 120 days. And he went into the ark, a son of 600 years and in the six hundred first year of his life, he went out from the ark in the month of Famount, according to the Egyptians, but according to the Hebrews, Nisan, on the 28th day. After the flood, he lived 350 years, and he died. He lived 950 years in all.(Melchizedek's appearance after the flood): "And when Abram heard that his brother was taken captive, he armed his trained servants, born in his own house, three hundred and eighteen, and pursued them unto Dan. And he divided himself against them, he and his servants by night, and smote them, and pursued them unto Hobah, which is on the left hand of Damascus. And he brought back all the good, and also brought again his brother Lot, and his goods, and the woman also, and the people. And the King of Sodom went out to meet him after his return from the slaughter of Chedorlaomer, and of the kings that were with him, at the valley of Shaveh, which is the king's dale. And Melchizedek, King of Salem, brought forth bread and wine: and he was the priest of El-Elyon. And he blessed him, and said, blessed be Abram of El-Elyon, possessor of heaven and earth: And blessed be El-Elyon, which hath delivered thine enemies into thy hand. And he (Abraham) gave him tithes of all."
Gen 14.14-20.

"For this Melchizedek, King of Salem, priest of Yahweh El-Elyon, who met Abraham returning from the slaughter of the kings, and blessed him; to whom also Abraham gave a tenth part of all; (first being by interpretation King of Righteousness, and after that also King of Salem or Peace); whose father and mother were not recorded in the genealogies, as such, neither the beginning of his days, nor the end of his life; but being a representation of the Son of Yahweh for the continuance for the priesthood. Now consider how great this man was, unto whom even the patriarch Abraham gave the tenth of the spoils." Heb. 7.1-10.

The blessing upon Abraham by Melchizedek, the first high priest of Yahweh El-Elyon, the Most High Power of Powers, perfected his spiritual walk and prepared him to be the father of a multitude of nations. And when Abram was ninety years old and nine, Yahweh appeared to Abram, saying,

"I am El-Shaddai, walk before Me and be perfect. And I will make my covenant between me and thee, and I will multiply thee exceedingly.' And Abram fell on his face; and Elohim talked with him, saying, `As for me, behold, my covenant* is with thee, and thou shall be a father of a multitude of nations. Neither shall thy name anymore be called Abram,

---

* (Covenant = an agreement that Yahweh makes with a man or a nation in relationship to His Divine Will, Jer. 31.31-33).

but thy name shall be Abraham; for a father of a multitude of nations have I made thee. And I will establish my covenant between Me and thee and thy seed after thee in their generation for an everlasting covenant, to be Elohim unto thee and to thy seed after thee." Gen 17.1-7.

According to the prophetic promise, this great man, Melchizedek, was foretold that there would come one of twelve High Priests who would rise up after him to fulfill the office and the teachings of the last priestly order through the seed of Abraham. Yahoshua (Jesus) was the promised holy seed foretold of who would come from the genealogy of Abraham to become the propitiation of the order of Melchizedek.

"For if the blood of bulls and of goats, and the ashes of an heifer sprinkling the unclean, sacrifice for the purifying of the flesh: How much more for the blood of Yahoshua, who through the eternal spirit, offered himself without blemish to Yahweh El-Elyon, purge your conscience from death, causing works to serve the living Elohim? And for this purpose He is the mediator of the New Covenant, that by means of death, for the redemption of transgressions of the first Covenant, those which are called might receive the promise of eternal inheritance." Hebrews 9.13-15.

Around the year 3 A.C.E., the fulfillment of the promise divinely given to Abraham, took place through the birth of a Hebrew child by a virgin woman named Mary (Miriam).

She called the child Yahoshua, which literally means Yahweh Delivers, according to instructions given by the Angel Gabriel. This child was destined to be the first of the twelve last high priests after the Order of Melchizedek. For every high priest taken from among me is ordained for men in things pertaining to Yahweh, that he may offer both gift and sacrifice for sin: Who can have compassion on the ignorant, and on them that are out of the way; for that he himself also is compassed with infirmity. And by reason he ought, as for the people, so also for himself to offer for sins. And no man taketh this honor unto himself, but he that is called of Yahweh as was Aaron. So also, the Messiah glorified not Himself to be made a high priest; but that said unto Him 'though art my son, today have I begotten thee' As He saith also in another place *'Though art a priest forever after the order of Melchizedek.'*

> *"Who in the days of his flesh, when he had offered up prayers and supplication with strong crying and tears unto Him that was able to save him from death, and was heard for His reverences; though he was the son, yet he learned obedience by the things he had suffered; which having accomplished, He became the author of eternal salvation unto them that obey Him; called of Yahweh a High Priest after the order of Melchizedek. Of whom we have many things to say, and hard to be uttered, seeing ye are dull of hearing. For when the time you ought to be teachers, ye have need that one teach you again which be the first principles of the oracles of Yahweh; and are become such as have need of milk, and not of strong meat. For every one that uses milk is unskillful in the word of righteousness: for he is a babe. But strong meat belongeth to them that are of full age, even those who by reason of use*

have their senses exercised to discern both good and evil." Hebrews 5.1-14.

"Wherein Yahweh, more abundantly to show unto the hires of promise the immutability of His counsel, confirmed it by an oath: "That by two immutable things in which it was impossible for Yahweh to lie, we might have a strong consultation, who have fled for refuge to lay hold upon the hope set before us: Which hope we have as an anchor of the soul, both sure and steadfast, and which entered into that within the veil; Wither the forerunner is for us entered, even Yahoshua, made a High Priest forever after the order of Melchizedek." Heb. 6.17-20.

נבי- Nabi (or Navi) = Prophet, Seer, Mouthpiece

Associated Words:

(לבוא) La-voe = to bring, come, arrive, enter, reach, come to pass, happen

(להביא) Le-Ha-Vee (verb) = To bring, bring about, to cause, lead, reduce (clarity)

The Author Nabi Melchizedek: The ancient Melchizedek, as the high priest to El-Elyon, was the teacher of the Holy Names of Yahweh and taught Abraham the use of these names: how to invoke and convoke the Holy Presence of the Most High Creator, Yahweh, to bring about blessings, power and change in his life. The lineage of these teachings was passed down from generation to generation, unto Moses, who wrote the Holy Names in the Hebraic Torah (Bible) and used the powers of the Holy Name to deliver the Children of Israel out of bondage. (In the scriptures the `rod of Moses' was the allegoric term for the use of the Holy Names).

Prophetically, while upon Mount Okeanu (the Mountain of Mercy) in Nigeria, West Africa, in the year 1975, on the15th day and the 26th day of January, I was divinely visited by a host of angels in front of fourteen people and was told that before I was in my mother's womb, I was fashioned and formed by Yahweh El-Elyon as a Holy Name Prophet unto Himself. I was also told that I was a King of Righteousness. After many years of praying and fasting, I have arrived at the understanding that my name, spirit and calling is identical to that of the ancient King Priest Melchizedek: my charge is to teach the wisdom of His Holy Names and to cause the Sons of Light to understand the Ages of Ages. To aid man in his upliftment and to overcome every obstacle spiritually mentally and physically.

TETRAGRAMMATON

> *"YAHWEH: He who can rightly pronounce it causeth heaven and earth to tremble, for it is the name which rusheth through the universe."* Fabre D'Olivet, The Hebraic Tongue Restored.

> *"And in all things that I have said unto you, be circumspect: and make no mention of the name of other Elohim, neither let it be heard out of thy mouth."* Ex. 23.13.

The Tetragrammaton or the four fold process is properly pronounced 'YAHWEH,' the original Hebraic Name of the Creator. *(See Introduction):*

The four-fold process of the Holy Name, is the key that opens the door to the Kingdom of Heaven. (John 10.9, 5.43, Rev. 3.7-13). The four letters, Yod-Hay-Waw-Hay, that make the Holy Name of Yahweh, are also a formula describing the universal process, (see Mark 4.11, John 1.1-12, Rev. 10.7):

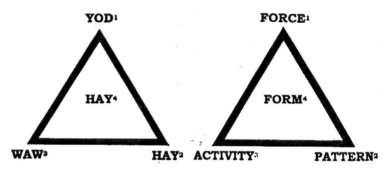

(**ʼ**) **Yod** - symbolized by the hand and represents the principle of force. It is the simplest in construction of all the Hebrew letters; it is the fundamental unit by which the other letters are formed; it symbolizes a flame, is masculine, active, and creative; it is the principle of force.

(**ה**) **Hay** - symbolized by a window, represents the principle of reception. Hay is feminine, passive, and acts as the container or formative principle with respect to Yod. Hay is the principle of pattern.

(ו) **Waw** - symbolized by a Peg, is the activity of Force (Yod) moving through the Receiving character of Hay, to Waw, the principle of activity.

(ה) **Hay** - the Window, is repeated as a fourth and last letter of the tetragrammaton. Here it indicates a pattern or structure which is the result of the first three letters acting as one, the second hay indicates manifestation of form.

The four aspects of the tetragrammaton are symbolized by the four elements, Fire, Water, Air and Earth. A simple example of the Tetragrammaton (three acting as one manifestation - four), is the process whereby electricity produced: the force (electricity) moving through a pattern (wire) causing activity (current flowing) which results in form, - the production of light:

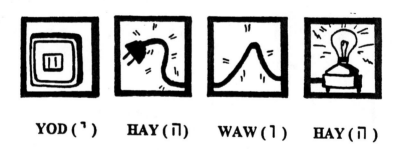

YOD (י)   HAY (ה)   WAW (ו)   HAY (ה)

Kabbalists have made many attempts to formulate the process by which existence came into manifestation. All fail, because it is impossible to fully encapsulate the Divine in metaphysics. However, mystics have never ceased to attempt such efforts, or to find them useful. In the version shown here the AYIN leaves a void in which the Divine Will manifests ten Divine Attributes. Will is visualized as a beam of light traveling inward from the periphery of Eternal Light to call forth, create, form and make the initial manifestation of the Divine, which is Atsilutic, the World of Emanation (Zimzum or Contraction; the first manifestation).

The Shem Ha Boreh, the special Name of Elohim given to Moses, can be seen, in a vertical arrangement, as the likeness of Adam Kadmon, the Primordial Man. The Hebrew letters, Yod-Hay-Waw-Hay, are perceived as representing not only the Divine Will, Intellect, Emotion and Action, but the four levels of Emanation, Creation, Formation and making, set out in three Pillars of Will, Mercy and Severity. This figure of the Kavod or Divine Glory, composed of black and white fire, is spoken of in Ezekiel as 'the appearance of a man.' (The Divine Name as Adam Kadmon).

79

In essence, the Almighty Creator has only one Holy Name properly called Yahweh and cannot be translated into another language:

> *"Fill their faces with shame; that they may seek thy name, Oh Yahweh. Let them be confounded and troubled forever; Yea, let them be put to shame, and perish: that they may know that thou, whose name alone is Yahweh El-Elyon over all the earth."* *Psalms 83.16-18.*

> *"And Yahweh shall be king over all the earth: And in that day Yahweh will prove to be a unity, and with one name."* *Zech. 14.9.*

It is important to call upon the name of the Creator in Hebrew because each letter of the Hebrew Aleph Beit (alphabet), twenty-two in number, is a spiritual force, a divine intelligence, a powerful energy, and a holy emanation. The letters are immutable forces that can never be destroyed. When Elohim combined them into words, phrases, and commands, they brought about creation; the elements of fire, water, and air came into being through the force of these letter energies. The Aleph Beit is the seed from which all physical expression took root and developed. These characters can be likened to living, breathing entities which, if used correctly, approached with faith, meditation and reverence, can link us with the vast spiritual universe, and facilitate a transformation of our reality in the physical realm.

Gematria of the Aleph Beit:

*"Yahweh by wisdom hath founded the earth;
by understanding hath established the
heavens. By his knowledge the depths are
broken up and the clouds drop down to the
dew." Pro. 3.19-20*

*"In the beginning was the word (the 22
letters of the Aleph Beit) and the Word was
with Yahweh, and the Word was Yahweh.
The same was in the beginning with Yahweh.
All things were made by him; and without
him was not anything that was made." John
1.1-3.*

The Zohar tells us that Eloha's (singular form for the
Almighty Creator) first creation in the endless worlds were
22 letters of the Hebrew Aleph Beit, but these letters were
far more than simple literal symbols of communication for
printers galley of type. They were, and are, living,
intelligent entities of unsurpassed beauty and wisdom -
Yahweh Eloha's blueprint for that which was to be made
manifest, and one of them would become the channel by
which He would create His multifaceted universe.

The letter, like their Creator, could see the future, for in
the endless world there is no time, space or motion.
Eternity is but a moment of comprehension of Yahweh El
Elyon.[3]

Only Yahweh Eloha's beloved letters would be fit as the
tools of His mighty thought. Yahweh Eloha spoke the
Word (John 1.1-2) and said 'be,' and the letter word went
forth and created the cosmos that propelled the

metaphysical unseen into the realm of the material reality world of today, through the energy of electrons.*

In the universe, (`ha olam'), there was created a positive and a negative energy connected by a resister which caused a live magnetic electrical circuit of electrons and many other trons for all Creation to receive. The negative side of the energy force was given the name desire (ratsone) to receive for one's self alone, the positive - as desire (ratsone) - to receive for the purpose of sharing.

An idea is the development of psycho energy universal systems, which is the structure of matter, not independent of consciousness. What must occur when consciousness affects matter: When a person does a good deed, he makes manifest and acquires a personal positive intelligent life force. All essence within our universe has been structured by the actions of man.

> *"For I reckon that the sufferings of this present time are not worthy to be compared with the glory which shall be revealed in us. For the earnest expectation of the creation waiteth for the manifestation of the Sons of Yahweh. For the creation was made subject to vanity, not willingly but by reason of him who hath subjected the same in hope. Because the creation itself also shall be*

---

*("Electron = an elementary particle consisting of a charge of negative electricity equal to about 1,602 x 10 coulombs and having a mass when at rest of abut 9,107 x 10 gram or 1/1837 that of a proton," Websters Collegiate Dictionary).

delivered from the bondage of corruption
into the glorious liberty of the children of
Yahweh. For we know that the whole
creation groaneth and travail- eth in pain
together until now." Rom. 8.18-22.

From even man's words of mouth are created angelic, metaphysical life forces.

"But I say unto you that every idle word that
men shall speak, they shall give account of it
in the day of judgment." Matt. 12.36.

But when we get down into the substance of that which we perceive as solid, physical reality, we return to the basic building block of nature - the electron. The Hebrew word for universe is 'Olam,' however, the root meaning of this word is concealment.

Each one of the 22 letters is a seed, a starting point on the path toward the most pure divine spiritual consciousness (Yahweh El-Elyon), who resides in four primary universes known and remembered as `Aviyah' (Father Yah).

The Zohar declares that Yahweh Eloha created two basic constellations. Each one consisted of four worlds. An equal cosmic power of good and evil was granted to these two constellations respectively. These worlds are referred to as 1) Atsilut (Emanation); 2) Briah (Creation); 3) Yitzerah (Formation), and 4) Asiyah (The action of liquids, gases and solids).

When these letter energies are called upon, they bring about changes of spiritual, mental and physical health.

While all intelligent energies must, of necessity; have been included within the base scope of the `endless' they become physically expressed through the letter energies. Which letters were responsible for and made manifest this cosmic energy? The Zohar answers: `from the living energy-intelligence (spirit) emanated air (spirit), water, and from water, fire.`

Of the 22 letters or inherent powers, including seven double and twelve simple consonants, three are the first elements. The Three fundamental elements were manifested by the letters Aleph, Mem and Shin, which form the basis for balance.

The Mem is mute like water and it makes manifest. Heaven was created from fire, the earth (sea and land) from water. The atmosphere established the balance among them. The three fundamental letter energies - Aleph, Mem and Shin - cause heat, coldness and moistness. Heat was created from fire, coldness from water and moistness from air which equalizes them.

The seven double letters: *Bet, Gimel, Dalet, Kaf, Pey, Resh and Tav,* were designed, established, combined, weighted and changed by Elohim. He formed from the seven planets in the universe, seven days in the year, representing the seven gates within the heavens, which correspond to the seven gates or senses in man, male and female.

Ancient astronomers recognized the seven planets in the universe to be Saturn, Jupiter, Mars, Sun, Venus, Mercury, and the Moon. The seven planets correspond to the seven days of the week, and to the seven gates in man, male and female: two eyes, two ears, two nostrils and mouth.

The Master infused the letter Beth with an intelligent energy-force by which to predominate in wisdom and formed the planet Saturn in the cosmos, the first day of the week, and the right eye in man. The Master infused the letter Gimel with an intelligent Energy-Force by which to predominate in peace, and He formed the planet Jupiter in the cosmos the second day of the week and the left eye in man.

The Master infused the letter Daleth with an intelligent energy-force by which to predominate in war and from the planet Mars in the cosmos, the third day of the week and the right ear of man. The Master infused the letter Kaph with an intelligent energy-force by which to predominate in reality, and He formed the Sun in the cosmos, the fourth day of the week, and the left ear in man.

The Master infused the letter Peh with an intelligent energy-force by which to predominate in love, and he formed the planet Venus in the cosmos, the fifth day of the week and the right nostril in man. The Master infused the letter Resh with an intelligent energy-force by which to predominate in the arts, and He formed the planet Mercury in the cosmos, the sixth day of the week, and the left nostril in man.

The Master infused the letter Tav with an intelligent energy-force by which to predominate in the kingdom, and he formed the planet Moon in the cosmos, the seventh day of the week and the mouth of man.

The remaining twelve letters were each provided with an intelligent energy-force by which to predominated in the constellations (the signs of the zodiac) to establish the twelve months in the year, twelve organs in the human body, male and female.

The twelve constellations in the cosmos are Aries, Taurus, Gemini, Cancer, Leo, Virgo, Libra, Scorpio, Sagittarius, Capricorn, Aquarius, and Pisces. The twelve months of the Hebrew year correspond to the twelve months of the Roman year. They are Nisan - March/April, Iyar - April/May, Sivan - May/June, Tammuz - June/July, Ab - July/August, Elul - August/September, Tishri - September/October, Masheshuan - October/November, Kislev - November/December, Tevet - December/January, Shebet - January/February, and Adar - February/March.

The twelve leaders of the human body are two hands, two feet, two kidneys, spleen, liver, gall bladder, stomach, the upper and lower intestines.

The Master infused the letter Hey with an intelligent energy-force by which to predominate and form Aries in the cosmos, Nisan in the year and the right hand in man. The same for the letter Waw to predominate in Taurus in the cosmos, Iyar in the year, and the left hand. The letter Zayin to predominate in Gemini in the cosmos, Sivan in the year and the right leg in man. The letter Heth to predominate in Cancer in the cosmos, Tammuz in the year and the left leg in man. The letter Teth to predominate in Leo in the cosmos, Maenabem Ab in the year and the right kidney in man. The letter Yod to predominate in Virgo in the cosmos, Elul in the year and the left kidney in man. The letter Lamed to predominate in Libra in the cosmos, Tishri in the year and liver in man. The letter Noon to predominate in Scorpio in the cosmos, Marheshuan in the year and the spleen in man. The letter Samekh to predominate in Sagitarius in the cosmos, Kislev in the year and the gall bladder in man. The letter Ayin to predominate in Capricorn in the cosmos, Teven in the year and the stomach in man. The letter Tsaday to predominate in Aquarius in the cosmos, Shebet in the year and the intestines in man. The letter Koof to predominate in Pisces in the cosmos, Adar in the year and the stomach in man.

The Aleph Beit consists of 10 numbers: 1, 2, 3, 4, 5, 6, 7, 8, 9, and 10. From these ten numbers all other numbers are formed. The Aleph Beit consists of 22 characters (originally 16), which are considered to be the foundation (Yesod) of the Cosmos. This foundation (Yesod) is called the square: $2 + 2 = 22$ or $2 + 2$ added together which is four. The square foundation is an ever-living witness to the Ameers (Amorites), Moors, Ethiopians, Egyptians, Mexicans, Olmecs, (all of whom were races of color), who built the pyramids of the world. The pyramid base is a square, having four sides.

The Aleph Beit key, the use of Gematria with the characters, is represented by the character Dahlet and can be turned in four different ways. Dahlet is symbolic of a Door (see chart, page 43). A door is designed to: 1) let things in, 2) let things out, 3) keep things in, 4) keep things out. Whenever these four keys are turned properly by using the science of Gematria numbers and alphabet, you will possess the same door or foundation upon which to build. John 10.9, I Cor. 3, 10, 17.

The ten gematria numbers, 22 characters of the Aleph Beit, and four keys, equal thirty-six paths of wisdom. 36 paths of wisdom ($10 + 22 + 4 = 36$) equals 9 levels ($3 + 6 = 9$). Nine is the complete or total level of the Cosmos principal initiation. By total 1 (one, achad, unity) means 360 or $3 + 6 + 0 = 9$ (Deut. 6.4).

Gematria is based on the relative numerical values of words. Words of similar numerical values are considered to be explanatory of each other and this theory is also extended to phrases.

THE HEBRAIC ALEPH BEIT:

Gematria is based on the relative numerical value of words. Words of similar numerical values are considered to be explanatory of each other and this theory is also extended to phrases:

Letter	Absolute value מספר הברחי
א	1 or 1000
ב	2
ג	3
ד	4
ה	5
ו	6
ז	7
ח	8
ט	9
י	10
ך,כ	20
ל	30
מ,ם	40
נ,ן	50
ס	60
ע	70
פ,ף	80
צ,ץ	90
ק	100
ר	200
ש	300
ת	400

Gimel ג	Vaht ב	Bayt בּ	Alef א
Zayin ז	Vavh ו	Hay ה	Dahlet ד
Cahph כ	Yeud י	Tet ט	Chet ח
Mem Sofit ם	Mem מ	Lamed ל	Cahph Sofit ך
Ayin ע	Samech ס	Nun Sofit ן	Nun נ
Tsaday צ	Fay Sofit ף	Fay פ	Pay פּ
Sheen שׁ	Resh ר	Koof ק	Tsaday Sofit ץ
Iseren Segol Kreek Potach Kamatz	Tahv ת	Seen שׂ	
Katof Shavah Sherook Khutz Kolom			

88

For example, the Hebrew words Achad (unity) and Ahavah (love), have the numerical value of 13. Also, the Angel of Metatron, who is said to have been the conductor of the children of Israel through the wilderness, and of whom Yahweh says, `My Name is in Him,' has the same numerical value as the Holy Attribute of the Creator termed `El-Shaddai,' or the Power Nourisher, Provider, Sustainer, each totaling 314. Each is therefore symbolic of the other. Each individual letter is a number and a force within itself. The same method of gematria should be applied to the holy attribute names of Yahweh to be invoked according to its numerical value. The numerical value of each of the twelve divine praise names have been divinely calculated by the Almighty Creator, Yahweh Elohim.

The 12 Divine Praise Names of Yahweh Elohim:

Name:	Meaning & Numerical Value:
Yahweh	*The Self-Existent One (26)*
יהוה	*The One Who Wills All Things to be*
Yahweh El-Elyon	*Yahweh is the Most High Power of Power*
יהוה אל עליון	*(128)*
Yahweh Tsebaote	*Yahweh is the Host or Armies of Heaven*
יהוה צבאות	*(499)*
Yahweh Nissi	*Yahweh is My Standard, My Banner, My*
יהוה נסי	*Test (120)*
Yahweh El-Roie	*Yahweh is My Seer, Spectator (237)*
יהוה רואי	
Yahweh El-Shaddai	*Yahweh is the Breasted One, Nourisher*
יהוה אל שדי	
Yahweh El-Olam	*Yahweh is The Everlasting Power (108)*
יהוה אל עולם	

Yahweh Will Provide (216)   Yahweh Yireh

יהוה ירה

Yahweh Khased   *Yahweh is Merciful, Kind, Loving (69)*

יהוה חסד

Yahweh Shalom   *Yahweh is Peace, Well-being, Safety,*

יהוה שלום   *Prosperity (376)*

Yahweh Rophekah   *Yahweh is Your Divine Healer (311)*

יהוה רופאך

Yahweh Roeh   *Yahweh is a Shepherd (281)*

יהוה רועה

Yahweh Tsedkanu   *Yahweh is Our Righteousness (250)*

יהוה צדקנו

El   *Strong, Mighty, Almighty Power*

אֵל

Elohim   *Almighty Creators*

אלוהים

According to the Zohar, the book of splendor, the days are approaching (in the prophetic time cycle, we are at the end of this age and approaching a New Age) when mankind will be able to tap the spiritual realms and gain access to the deeper mysteries of heaven and nature. In order to tap into these higher spiritual realms, we must invoke the Holy Presence to work on our behalf through calling upon His Holy Name(s) and Attributes as our forefathers did, from Melchizedek even unto the great King David:

> *"I cried with my whole heart; Hear me, Oh Yahweh, I will keep thy statutes. I cried unto thee. Save me, and I shall keep thy testimonies." Ps. 119.145-146*

90

"In my distress I cried unto Yahweh, and He heard me." Ps. 120.1

The English word `cried' or `to cry' is written as KARAH, in the original Hebraic text:

קְרָה

KAH-RAH = to read, to call (cry out), to proclaim, pronounce, preach, to name, call by name, to study (the Word), to recite, to summon, invite, assemble, convene, emplore.

קֹר

KAR, first primary root = The compressive sign united to that of movement proper, constitutes a root which develops the idea of that which is incisive, penetrating, firm, straight, that which engraves or which serves to engrave; every kind of engraving, character, or sign fitting to preserve the memory of things. From the idea of character and unity contained in this root has come that of reading and from reading that of every oratorical discourse spoken aloud; thence the divers expressions of crying out, exclaiming, speaking, proclaiming, reading, naming, designating a thing by name, by expedient sign; to convoke, evoke, etc.

The sign of movement proper (אר), united to that of power, forms a root characterized hierogriphically by the gematria radius: that is to say. By that kind of straight line which departing from the center converges at any point whatsoever of the circumference: it is, in a very restricted sense, a streak, in a broader sense, a ray and metaphorically, the visual ray, visibility. Action of seeing, fixing the eyes upon an object, beholding, considering; sight, vision, aspect of a thing.[5]

For any of the divine praises to be invoked, or called upon, there is a Holy Name attribute of Yahweh given by divine decree and sent to the earth to be the seal to all prophecy, invocation, prayer, and meditation.

Meditate on each of the attributes and use them according to your need; they are not simply names, but powers which can pierce through the worlds and open wide the gates of the heavens.

Yahweh Eloha, the Almighty Creator, is attributed into a multitude of manifestations, each with its own particular power, governing angels, and divine properties. In order to receive the greatest blessing from their usage, it is important to know what aspects of the Almighty Creator to call on. The invocation of each name brings about a particularly powerful result which you can witness in your life after applying intense and faithful application. Meditate upon each of the twelve divine praise names for each one is only a general synopsis of the profound significance of each name. It is important that the invocations be done using the Hebrew names because of the angelic powers associated with them. The English equivalent does not lend itself to the divine spiritual energy that is associated with the original Hebraic Tongue, which flows forth from the universe of the four worlds.

All of the names are an example of the Unity of the Creator, which many times is misinterpreted as different creators, but in reality is simply the differentiation of the Divine Attributes of the One Creator, the Unity of Yahweh.

YAHWEH - each attribute starts with Yahweh, because the vibration of the spoke word, Yahweh, brings about the will to be. Remember, in all the usage's you must apply faith.

1. YAHWEH EL-ELYON = Yahweh is the Most High Power of Powers, Elevated, Lofty. *Primary Root Word: Alah* עלה *to ascend, to be high, to mount, to rise up, to arise, to cause to ascend, to bring up, to cause to burn, carry up, cast up,, climb, to cause or make to come up, to exalt, excel, fetch up, grow, increase, lay, leap, levy, lift up, light, make up, to mount up, make to pay, recover, restore, scale, set up, shoot forth, spring up, stir up. Opposite = cut off, cut down, depart, fall.*

Usage: By calling upon this attribute of the Creator, you are calling upon the Generator and Source of all power, the Most High Power of Powers through whom all things are possible to them that believe.

2. YAHWEH TSEBAOTE = Yahweh is the Holy Army (Host) of Heaven. *Root Word: Tsavah (צבא)* = *army, host, troops; (verb) to assemble, congregate, gather together, wage war, to force.* That is, Yahweh is one with the Heavenly Host of Angels and Spiritual forces which have only one mind and are called to do the perfect ill of Yahweh.

Usage: If you have enemies, whether spiritual, mental or physical, this attribute called upon by faith, goes into embattlement for you against all unrighteous opposition. Be warned! You cannot use this attribute to work evil, for it is a righteous power and the misuse of it can cause the reverse action to the user.

3. YAHWEH NISSI - Yahweh is our Standard, Banner, Ensign, Signal, Warning, Flag. *Root Word, Nis* (נסי) = *Miracle, wonder, prodigy, marvel, providential, wonderful event. Root Verb: Niseh* (נסה) = *to try, examine, test, experiment, to tempt, attempt.*

Usage: This attribute activates the principle of moral standard. That is, if one is doing something of a low or immoral nature and desires a righteous change, he/she may call upon this attribute to help raise him or someone else up to a high standard of morality in consciousness and deed.

4. YAHWEH EL-ROIE = Yahweh, the Power of Vision. *Root Word, Roeh = Spectator, seer, prophet, visionary. Primary Verb, Ra-Ah* (ראה) = *To see, look at, behold, observe, regard, view, perceive, to understand, conceive, feel; to choose, prefer, approve of, reflect, look, see, witness, be witness to, consider, discern, enjoy, have* *experience, gaze, take heed, look on, perceive, present, provide, regard, meet, mark, respect, show, think, view, envision (or cause another to).*

Usage: This attribute invokes the All Seeing, All Knowing, Omnipotent Power of Yahweh. Therefore, one may call upon this divine attribute, the principle of Divine Sight, to give discernment to self or for Yahweh to perceive, regard or respect a prayer, a desire, a circumstance, event, etc..

5. YAHWEH EL-SHADDAI - The Nourisher, Owner, Sustainer of the Heavens and Earth, Breasted One, Almighty and All Sufficient Provider. *Root Words: a) `Shad'* (שד) *= Nipple, bosom; protuberance; affluence, source of blessings, b) "dai"* (די) *= adequacy, sufficiency, the requisite, plenty; enough, sufficiency.*

Usage: As a mother nourishes her newborn baby entering the natural world, so are we nurtured by the Spiritual Mother, Yahweh, as we are continually born and reborn upon the path of spiritual knowledge and truth. A mother has breasts to nurture the life of her newborn baby and to give it all of the sufficient properties that its body needs to sustain its life. So does the Spiritual Mother, Yahweh El-Shaddai, have all of the keys to nourish and provide our every need.

6. YAHWEH EL-OLAM - Yahweh is Everlasting. *Root Word, Olam* (עוֹלָם) = Everlasting, the Ancient of Days, World, Universe, Humanity, Space, Community, Existence, Surroundings, Assembly, Pleasure of life, Eternity, Ages, Distant Future, the Next World, the After Life, Always Continuance, Forever, Perpetual, World Without End.

Usage: Many times in life, we are faced with some problem or negative condition and we may have read or been told of how the prophets of old overcame every obstacle that confronted them. How did they do this? With the realization that there is nothing new under the sun, this attribute is the same today as it was yesterday. It is the same in the modern world as it was in the ancient world, as it will be in the world to come. The everlasting power, the King of the Universe, is what you invoke to help you overcome as the prophets of old overcame.

7. YAHWEH YIREH - Yahweh will Provide. *Root Word, Yarah* (ירה) = *to provide, shoot, fire; to throw; to pour, to teach, instruct, direct, show, decide, enjoin, command.*

Usage: When you desire the substance of anything and then begin to faithfully invoke Yahweh Yireh, the One who Wills All things to Be with His attribute of Provision (Yireh), the creative energy in you wills that which you ask for into existence.

8. YAHWEH CHASED = Yahweh is Merciful. Root Word, Chased (חסד) = merciful, kind, pious, beautiful, favored, loving, gracious, charitable, benevolent, good.

Usage: There are times in life when you may do something that requires you to ask for mercy, love and kindness from the Creator; but remember, to receive mercy from this attribute, you must be able to give mercy to others.

9. YAHWEH SHALOM = Yahweh is Peace. *Root Word: Shalam (שלם) = peace, safety, well-being, happiness, welfare, health, prosperity, success, favor, friendship, prosperity, tranquillity, calmness, security, rest, quiet. Related Word: Shalame = to be completed, finished, ended, intact ,integral, unhewn, full, perfect, total; safe, uninjured, unharmed, unscathed, healthy, true, faithful; peaceful.*

Usage: All people, righteous or evil, desire this attribute of peace. You may be troubled by many problems in your daily life and worry and unrest permeate your thoughts because you don't know how to handle them. By faithfully calling upon this attribute, you can restore the spirit of peace to your life under trying conditions.

10. YAHWEH ROPHEKAH = Yahweh is your Healer (Ps 103.3). *Root Word: Rofeh (רופאך) = to mend, cure, heal, repair thoroughly, make whole, remedy, (See Is 30.26, `Oh physician, heal thyself').*

Usage: We are living in an age of plagues, call them what you will. They are a result of sin - falling short of the will of Yahweh. When medical doctors have no healing methods and no power, Yahweh Rophekah, when called upon in faith, never fails, for this attribute is Forever.

11. YAHWEH ROEH = Yahweh is the Shepherd, herdsman, pastor, leader, guide. *Root Word, Ra-ah (רעה) = to tend (a flock), lead, guide, graze, pasture, follow, associate with, keep company, befriend, to rule, to be a companion, feed, keep, share the same cares; to be a neighbor, relative, comrade.*

Usage: Many people are familiar with the Biblical story of King David when he was a shepherd over a flock of sheep. He protected them against wolves and against the dangers of life. So, likewise, we may have fears for our loved ones or for ourselves, because of some threat or danger which we believe can affect our lives and harm us in some way. This attribute, when faithfully invoked, shepherds over our lives and we are safe.

12. YAHWEH TSIDKENU = Yahweh is our Righteousness. *Root Word, Tsadak (צדק) = to make right (in a moral or forensic sense), to cleanse; justice, righteousness, straightness, true honesty.*

Usage: *For those who desire righteousness and justice, this attribute is most potent to help one come to the standard of Yahweh and bring about the righteousness one desires under any condition.*

YAHOSHUA = Yah (Yahweh) will save, deliver, redeem, help. *Root Word: Yesha (ישע) = redemption, delivery, rescue, salvation. Primary Root: Sha-ah (שעה) = To turn to, gaze at, regard, pay heed, consider, notice, look about.*

Usage: This attribute is the vibration which seals all invocation and prayer. To ensure the effectiveness of your invocation or petition, call upon this attribute at the end of every prayer. Yahoshua means 'Yahweh will deliver or save.' The name Jesus, on the other hand, is a transliteration derived from the Greek god of Zeus, and does not project the true name and meaning of Yahoshua as it was given and written in the original Hebraic Bible:

"Wherefore Yahweh also hath highly exalted Him, and has given Him a name which is above every name: That at the name of Yahoshua, every knee should bow, of things in the heavens, and things in the

earth, and things under the earth; And that
every tongue should confess that Yahoshua
is the Messiah to the glory of Yahweh the
Father." Phillipians 2.9-11

The Alpha and Omega (Aleph and Tav in Hebrew), the
beginning and the seal of the end, is the name Yahoshua
(Yahweh is the Deliverer), of body, mind and soul, here
and now, as well as in the after life.

These are the true mysteries given to the faithful seeker of
truth in these last days of grace. The knowledge of the 12
divine praise names can only be manifested through the
development of PERFECT LOVE, for the Creator. This
perfect Love is demonstrated through doing His will,
keeping His laws, and serving mankind.

> *"And though I have the gift of prophesy, and*
> *understand all mysteries, and all knowledge;*
> *and though I have all faith, so that I could*
> *remove mountains, and have not love, I am*
> *nothing." I Cor. 13.2.*

> *"There is no fear in love; but perfect love*
> *casteth out fear: because fear hath torment.*
> *He that feareth is not made perfect in love.*
> *We love Him, because he first loved us. If a*
> *man say, I love Yahweh, and hateth his*
> *brother, whom he hath seen, how can he*
> *love Yahweh whom he hath not seen? And*
> *this commandment have we from Him, that*
> *he who loveth Yahweh, loveth his brother*
> *also." I John 4.18-20.*

"And in that day, ye shall ask Me nothing. Verily, Verily, I say unto you, whatever ye shall ask the Father in My Name, He will give it to you." John 16.23.

The prophet Daniel's prayers were held up for twenty one days by the powers of darkness and negativity, which are the powers of the air; therefore, you must have faith and `faint not`; you must be consistent until you see the effects of your desire made manifest in the Asiyah World (the World of Manifestation).

THE POWER OF PRAYER & INVOCATION

Positions of Prayer: Bowing, Prostrating, Kneeling, Stretching Out and Lifting of Hands:

1. *'To Prostrate Oneself'*: this word incorrectly appears in most versions of the King James Bible as 'to worship.' We have corrected the scriptural readings in this chapter to reflect the original and correct Hebrew word 'Heeshtachavah' meaning to prostrate oneself or to bow down:

השתחוה
(Hesh-Tah-Chah-Vah)   = to bow down, prostrate oneself

השתחויה
(Heesh-Tah-Chav-Yah)   = a bow, bowing down, prostration, making obeisance, genuflection

To Prostrate = 1) lying with the face downward in demonstration of great humility or abject submission; 2) lying flat, prone, or supine 3) thrown or fallen to the ground; 4) laid low. (Webster's New World Dictionary, Third College Edition).

2. *'To bow'* or *'Kadad'* as it appears in the Hebrew text of the Bible, is defined as follows

קָדַד

(Kah-Dahd) = to bow, bend

קָדָה

(Kah-Dah) = to bow, bob, curtsey

3. *'To kneel'* or *'Barach'* as it appears in the Hebrew text of the Bible, is defined as follows:

בָּרַךְ

(Bar-rach) = to kneel, bend the knee, genuflect

4. 'To *Stretch Out'* the Hands or *'Parash'* as it appears in the Hebrew text, is defined as follows:

פָּרַשׂ

(Parash) = to spread, cast (net), stretch out, expand, extend, unfurl

5. *'To Lift Up'* the Hands or *'Moal'* as it appears in the Hebrew text, is defined as follows

מוֹעַל

(Moh-ahl) =   lifting, raising
(Mah-ahl)   = upward, high, aloft, heaven
(Ah-lah) = to go up, ascend, to rise, be lifted up

Lifting up of Hands followed by Prostration
& Bowing Down:

"And Ezra blessed Yahweh, the Great Elohim, and all the people responded 'So be it' ('Amen') with lifting up of hands: and they bowed and prostrated themselves with their faces to the ground." Nehemiyah 8:6

Prostration & Bowing preceed Kneeling & Lifting Up of Hands:

"Oh come, let us prostrate ourselves and bow down: Let us kneel before Yahweh, our Maker."
Psalms 95.6.

Bowing and Prostration were used in former times as gestures of praise, thanks, blessing, and to represent great humility and obedience. Bowing and Prostration may be used prior, subsequent to or throughout one's prayer and invocation.

'The Stretching Out of the Hands' toward Jerusalem or the Temple in Jerusalem and the 'Lifting Up of the Hands' towards Heaven in conjunction with the body posture of standing or kneeling, were the Standard Prayer and Invocation Positions of the Children of Israel. (See illustration). The Lifting up and Stretching Out of hands were used for prayer and invocation as well as to express Praise, Thanks, to give Blessings, to Heal, to Affirm or Will a Matter (i.e. 'So Be it'/'Amen').

Many Keys to Effective Prayer were revealed by the Great King Solomon in His Prayer for Physical and Spiritual Israel and for the Temple which He built for the Glory of the Holy Name of Yahweh:

> *"And now, O Elohim of Israel, let thy word, I pray thee, be verified, which thou spakest unto thy servant David, my father. But will Elohim indeed dwell on the earth? Behold, the heaven and the heaven of heavens cannot contain thee; how much less this house that I have built? Yet have thou respect unto the prayer of thy servant, and to his supplication:* **O Yahweh, My Elohim, to hearken unto the cry and to the prayer which thy servant prayeth before thee today: That thine eyes may be opened toward this house night and day, even toward the place of which thou hast said,**

'My Name shall be there': **that thou mayest hearken to the prayer which thy servant shall make toward this place: And hearken Thou to the supplication of thy servant, and of thy people, Israel, when they shall pray toward this place:** *and hear Thou in heaven Thy dwelling place: and when Thou hearest forgive.*

If any man tresspass against his neighbor, and an oath be laid upon him to cause him to swear, and the oath come before Thine alter in this house, Then hear Thou in heaven, and do, and judge Thy servants, condemning the wicked, to bring his ways upon his head; and justifying the righteous, to give him according to his righteousness. When Thy people Israel, be smitten down before the enemy, because they have sinned against Thee, and shall turn again to Thee, and **confess Thy Name,** *and pray and make supplication unto Thee in this house, then hear Thou in heaven, and forgive the sin of Thy people Israel, and bring them again unto the land which Thou gavest unto their fathers. When heaven is shut up, and there is no rain, because they have sinned against Thee;* **if they pray toward this place, and confess Thy Name and turn from their sin,** *when Thou afflictest them, Then hear Thou in heaven, and forgive the sin of Thy servants, and of thy people, Israel, that Thou teach them the good way wherein they should walk, and give rain upon Thy land, which Thou has given to Thy people for an inheritance.*

If there be in the land famine, if there be pestilence, blasting, mildew, locust, of if there be caterpillar; if their enemy besiege them in the land of their cities, whatsoever plague, whatsoever sickness there be; whatsoever prayer and supplication be made by any man or by all Thy people Israel, which shall know every man the plague of his own heart, and **spread forth his hands toward this house***: Then hear Thou in heaven, Thy dwelling place, and forgive and do, and give to every man according to his ways, whose heart Thou knowest; (for Thou, even Thou only, knowest the heart of all the children of men;) That they may fear Thee all the days that they live in the land which Thou gavest unto our fathers.*

Moreover, concerning a stranger, that is not of thy people Israel, but cometh out of a far country for Thy Name's sake; for they shall hear of Thy Great Name, and of Thy Strong Hand, and of Thy Stretched-out Arm; when he shall come and pray toward this house; Hear Thou in heaven Thy dwelling place, and do according to all that the stranger calleth to Thee for: That all people of the earth may know Thy Name, to fear Thee, as do Thy people Israel; and that they may know that this house which I have built is called by Thy Name.

If Thy people go out to battle against their enemy, wither soever Thou shalt send them, and shall pray unto Yahweh toward *the city which thou hast chosen and toward the house that I have built for Thy Name: Then hear Thou in heaven, their prayer and their supplication, and maintain their cause. If they sin against Thee, for there is no man that sinneth not, and Thou be angry with them, and deliver them to the enemy, so that they carry them away captives unto the land of the enemy, far or near; and **if they have a change of heart in the land where they are held captive, and repent and plead with you in the land of their conquerors saying, 'we have sinned and done perversely, we have committed wickedness; And so return unto Thee with all their heart, and with all their soul, in the land of their enemies, which led them away captive, and pray unto Thee toward their land**, which Thou gavest unto their fathers, the City which Thou hast chosen, and the house which I have built for Thy Name: Then hear Thou their prayer and their supplication in heaven, Thy dwelling place, and maintain their cause, and forgive Thy people that have sinned against Thee, and all their transgressions wherein they have transgressed against Thee, and give them compassion before them who carried them away captive, that they may have compassion on them.*

And it was so, that when Solomon made an end of praying all these prayers and supplications unto Yahweh, he arose from before the altar of Yahweh, from kneeling on his knees with his hands spread up to heaven." *I Kings 8:26-50*

109

"That Yahweh appeared to Solomon the second time, as He had appeared unto him at Gibeon. And Yahweh said unto him, **'I have heard thy prayer and thy supplication that thou hast made before me: I have hallowed this house, which thou hast built, to put My Name there forever; and mine eyes and my heart shall be there perpetually."** *I Kings* 9:2-3.

According to the covenant King Solomon made with Yahweh El Elyon, Yahweh placed his Name in the Temple built by Solomon and His Eyes were opened toward the Temple and City of Jerusalem night and day in order that He would hear prayers of his servants. The hearing of one's prayer by the Creator was contingent upon one's fulfillment of certain actions identified by King Solomon in the above prayer as: Praying toward (facing) the Temple or toward Jerusalem (if outside of Israel);

- Spreading forth their hands toward the Temple or toward Jerusalem if outside Israel;

Confessing The Name of Yahweh; [The word 'Confess' •
(Hodoo) from the root Yadah הודו is written in Hebrew which means 'to admit, confess; acknowledge, ידה thank, glorify, praise.' Therefore, this passage can also be read, 'Acknowledge or Praise the Name of Yahweh.'

- Changing one's heart (mind; state of mind; mentality) in the land where they are held captive;

- Repentance (Turning from sin; returning to the ways of the Creator) and Pleading (asking for mercy) of Yahweh in the lands of captivity saying, 'we have sinned and done perversely, we have committed wickedness'; *Repent, (Shoov) = to return, come back; revert, be transformed, repeat, do again; go back. To Ask for Mercy (Heet-chah-nan) = to ask for mercy, entreat, implore, beseech, beg, supplicate.*

- And returning to Yahweh with all their heart, and with all their soul (in the land of their enemies).

At the end of King Solomon's Prayer and of his completion of the building of the temple, Yahweh appeared to him and revealed that he heard his prayer. II Chron. 7.11-22. As with all covenants between the Creator and Israel, it was contingent upon Israel's obedience. However, the prayer itself, which Yahweh heard or obeyed, included a plan of redemption in the case of Israel's disobedience and consequent captivity. (See above verses).

יהוה

Invocation: Yod-Hay-Waw-Hay

<u>Position One:</u>

י (YOD)

"And I bowed down and prostrated before Yahweh, and blessed Yahweh-Elohim of my master Abraham, who led me in the right way to take my master's brother's daughter unto his son." Abraham's servant, Genesis 24:46

Position One:

' (YOD)

As seen in the 'Yod' illustration (page 64), for the First Position, the body is formed into the shape of the first letter of the Tetragrammaton, Yod, by bending the head and upper body forward in a forty-five degree angle with the hands at the sides. While in this position, the person prayer chants or sings the name of the letter Yod. As stated in the earlier chapter, the Yod symbolizes a flame; it is masculine, active and creative and represents the principle of force. The pathway of the Yod is the initial point of space and time and brings about natural wisdom: it directs on into the consciousness of the present moment. It forces of the principle of action and reaction into the wave of nature and of spiritual radiation.

When one places themselves in the Position of Yod, it will assist in opening the Chakras of the crown and upper body by activating the flow of the energy force to those areas.

Position Two:

ה (HAY)

"And David said to all the congregation, 'Now bless Yahweh, your Elohim.' And all the congregation blessed Yahweh Elohim of their fathers, and bowed and prostrated themselves to Yahweh and the King." I Chronicles 29:20.

Position Two:

ה (HAY)

Demonstrated the 'Position Two' illustration, the second position, Hay, is formed by maintaining the upper body in the Yod body position and stretching the arms straight toward the ground. Using the voice, the character Hay is vocalized in the same manner that the Yod was vocalized. Hay is feminine, passive, and acts as the container of formative principle with respect to Yod. Hay is the principle of pattern and causes the dimension of reality to elevate beyond the initial perception of the sense, emanating and transcending light, perceiving divine revelation and beholding Yah.

Third Position:

ו (WAW)

"And he stood before the altar of Yahweh in the presence of all the congregation of Israel and spread out his hands." II Chronicles 6:12.

"When Solomon had made an end of praying all this prayer and supplication unto Yahweh, he arose from before the altar of Yahweh, from kneeling on his knees with his hands spread up towards the heaven." I Kings 8.54

Third Position:

ו (WAW)

The third position, Waw, is formed by standing erect and stretching the hands upward toward the heavens. Simultaneously, the Waw is vocalized as the Yod and Hay were vocalized with a chant or song. Waw is the activity of Yod (Force) moving through the pattern of Hay. Waw is the principle of activity. Waw is the connecting road to the heavenly tabernacle, the complete stature of man standing on earth with his head reaching up toward the heavens. It is the activity of force connecting the divine spark inherent throughout reality.

Fourth Position:

ה (HAY)

"And the people believed and when they heard that Yahweh had visited the Children of Israel, and that He had looked upon their affliction, then they bowed and prostrated themselves." Exodus 4:31

Fourth Position:

ה (HAY)

(Repeat the Second Position, 'Hay'). The Second Hay, the fourth letter of the Tetragrammaton, the four letters that spell the Holy Name of Yahweh, indicates the manifestation of form; the first three letters (Yod, Hay, Waw) acting as one united force; thought, speech and action acting as one united force, and causes one to behold the revelations manifested in each of the three dimensions of reality.

After invoking each character of the Holy Name, Yod-Hay-Waw-Hay, separately, you may assume one of the positions of prostration, as demonstrated in the illustration below, followed by an invocation of any the of the Divine Praise Names of Yahweh (See Chapter on the Tetragrammaton) and your petition, prayer or supplication.

This system of invocation is one of the great spiritual keys to unlocking the gates and windows of heaven, in order that your prayers may be effectively heard.

SHEM-HA-BOREH

The 72 Angels Bearing the Name of the Creator:

(מלאך) MALACH = Angel, delegate, messenger, herald; (also) prophet

The 72 Malakim bearing the Holy Name of the Creator in the form of 'El' (The Strong One; Strength; Power) or 'Yah' (The Self Existing One) are Powers or Messengers appointed by Yahweh El Elyon which rule over the hosts of heaven and are responsible for initiating certain works to be performed on behalf of Yahweh and the Sons and Daughters of Light.

These Messengers were created by Yahweh to work on His behalf and given various portions and degrees of His Spiritual Attributes. These Messengers - 144 in all - are organized in two assemblies: The 72 Greater Holy Assembly, ruling over the sixth through the twelfth heaven, and the 72 Lesser Holy Assembly, ruling over the first through the sixth heaven (Makon).

The Holy Spirit is the key which unlocks the power of these divine names. Although you can call upon any of these 72 names once and be heard, according to your level of faith or the number of previous invocations, the full power of each name is achieved when you call upon them according to their gematria equivalent.

With the great voice, the inner spirit, or the quite sound of a whisper, each one of these attributes are to be gematriaally invoked in a state of meditation; as the vibration of pure thought and sound goes forward the spirit of Yahweh working through that celestial being will be enacted on your behalf. Your invocation should be followed by your request or petition of that divine angel or messenger to manifest itself or its holy virtues on your behalf in a comprehensible form of peace.

1)   Name: **VEHUYAH (Ve-hoo-Yah)**
       Meaning: *'And He is Yah'*
       Etimology: והו = and He is
                    יה = the self existent one

Gematria Sum: 32
Position & Service: A Celestial Messenger (Angel) who is called upon to realize prayer, governs the first rays of the sun and is one of the eight Seraphim.

2)   Name: **YAHLIEL (Yah-lee-El)**
           Meaning: *Yah is My Strength*
           Etimology: ילי = Yah is to me
                            אל = the Power

Gematria Sum: **86**
Position & Service: Governs future events.

3)   Name: **SITAEL (See-Tah-El)**
           Meaning: *Deflection/Diversion of El*
           Etimology: סטה = Deflection, diversion
                            יה = the self existent one

Gematria Sum: **110**
Position & Service: One of the eight Seraphim and one of the 72 rulers of the zodiac; governs Nobility and is invoked to conquer adversity.

4)   Name: **ELEMIYAH (Eh-lem-Yah)**
           Meaning: *The Secret/Youth of Yah*
           Etimology: עלם = Secret; Youth
                            יה = the self existent one

Gematria Sum: **155**
Position & Service: One of the eight Seraphim who rules over the Tree of Life, Voyages and Sea travel.

5)   Name: **MAASIYAH (Mah-ah-see-Yah)**
           Meaning: *Activity/Action/Labor of Yah*

           Etimology: מעסה = action, activity, art, business, deed, labor, act, doing, operation.
                            יה = the self existent one

Gematria Sum: **425**

Position & Service: *One of the 72 Angels bearing the Shem Ha Boreh.*

6)   Name: **LELAEL (Le-Lah-El)**

Position & Service: *One of the Celestial Messengers of the Zodiac who has dominion over art, science and future events.*

7)   Name: **AEHAYAH (Ay-hay-YAH)***

Position & Service: *One of the 72 Angels bearing the Shem Ha Boreh*

8)   Name: **CAHETEL (Cah-het-EL)**
    Meaning: *The Healing/Cure/Remedy of El*
    Etimology: כהט = Healing, Cure, Remedy
        or Ceehah = To rebuke, upbraid, admonish, reprove (i.e. in order to heal the land or body, weeds/evil/ sickness must be uprooted)

Gematria Sum: **476**
Position & Service: One of the Eight Seraphim who governs agricultural products, summoned to augment/improve crops.

9)   Name: **HAZIEL (Hah-Zee-EL)**
    Meaning: *Vision/Perception of El*
    Etimology: Hazah (חזה) = To Dream, visualize, percieve
        Hazayah (חזיה)= Dream, vision, perception
        El (אל) = Strength; The Strong One

Gematria Sum: 53

Position & Service: *A Cherubim evoked to receive the mercy of Elohim, i.e. Elohim percieves me or my condition.*

10) Name: **ALADYAH (Ah-lahd-YAH)**

    Meaning: *Yah Will Bring Forth*

    Etimology: ילד = To bear, bring forth, gather, procreate, reproduce

              עלד = To asist in Birth; midwife

              יה = the self existent one

Gematria Sum: 50

Position & Service: *One of the 72 Messengers bearing the Shem Ha Boreh*

11) Name: **LAVYAH (Lahv-Yah)**

Gematria Sum: 52

Position & Service: *One of the 72 Messengers bearing the ShemHaBoreh*

12) Name: **HAHIYAH (Hah-Hee-Yah)**

    Meaning: *Alas! It is Yah!*

    Etimology: Hah (הַ)_= Woe; Alas; Ah

              Hee (הי) = It; She

              Yah (יה) = The Self Existing One

Gematria Sum: 95

Position & Service: *This Messenger dwells within the order of the Cherubim, influences thought and hidden mysteries.*

13) **Name:**   **LAYLAEL (Ly-lah-EL)**
    Meaning: *El (Power) of the Night*
    Etimology: לילה = Night, darkness;

Gematria Sum: **81**
Position & Service: *Guardian Ruler of the Night.*

14) **Name:**   **MEBAEL (Meh-Bah-EL)**
    Meaning: *From Amongst EL (Power)*
    Etimology: מ = from, of, more than, since
    ב =_ in, among, within, into, with, by, through, because of
    אל = Strength; The Strong One

Gematria Sum: **78**
Position & Service: *One of the 72 Messengers of the Shem Ha Boreh*

15) **Name:**   **HARIEL (Har-ee-EL)**
    Meaning: *Concieve/Create El (Power)*
    Etimology: הרה = to concieve, create; impregnate
    אל = Strength; The Strong One

Gematria Sum: **246**
Position & Service: *A member of the Order of the Cherubim who rules over science and art, has dominion over animals; evoked against unrighteousness.*

16) **Name:**   **HAKAMYAH (Hah-Kahm-YAH)**
    Meaning: *The Setting Up/Establishment of Yah*
    Etimology: הקם = erection, setting up, keeping, construction,

establishment, foundation,
reconstruction, assembly

יה = the self existent one

Gematria Sum: **78**
*Position & Service: A member of the Order of Cherubim
who is evoked against traitors and is the Guardian
Messenger (Malahk) of France*

17) Name: **LEVIYAH**
     Meaning: *The Auxiliary/Ornament of Yah*
     Etimology: לוי = Attachment, Ornament
                  יה = The Self Existing One

Gematria Sum: **52**
*Position & Service: One of the 72 Angels bearing the
                       Shem Ha Boreh.*

18) Name: CEHLIEL (Ceh-Lee-EL)
     Meaning: *The Weapon of EL*
     Etimology: כלי = Weapon, instrument,
                  article, thing, vessel, utensil, tool,
                  organ, apparatus
                  כלה = Extinction, extermination,
                  annihilation, destruction,
                  determination, entirely, completely,
                  altogether.
                  יה = the self existent one

Gematria Sum: **91**
*Position & Service: This Messenger is evoked to summon
assistance against adversity & serves in The second heaven
(Raqia) (Rakiah).*

19) Name: **LEUYAH (Leh-ooh-YAH)**
    Meaning: *Yah and I (United with Yah)*

Position & Service: One of the 72 Angels bearing the
                        Shem Ha Boreh.

20) Name: **PAAHLIYAH (Pah-ah-Lee-Yah)**
    Meaning: *Yah Accomplishes/Acts/Influences*
    Etimology: פעל = To do, make, achieve,
    perform, accomplish, work, act,
    create, form, influence.
    יה = the self existent one

Gematria Sum: **195**
Position & Service: *This Messenger is evoked to
influence others toward righteousness/performing the Will
of Elohim, and governs Morality.*

21) Name: **NELCHAEL (Nel-cah-EL)***

Position/Service: *A Member of the Order of Thrones
who teaches astronomy, mathmatics and geography; also
of the fallen Messengers (Angels) in Sheol (Hell).*

22) Name: **YEHYAHEL (Yeh-YAH-EL)***

Position/Service: A Malahk of the Future.

23) Name: **MELAHEL (Mee-Lah-EL)**
    Meaning: *Command/Word of El*
    Etimology: מלה =_Word, command,
    speaking, matter, thing.
    אל = Strength; The Strong One

Gematria Sum: **106**

Position/Service: *One of the 72 Angels bearing the*
                                 Shem Ha Boreh.

24)   Name: **HAHUYAH (Ha-hoo-YAH)***

Position/Service: *One of the 72 Angels bearing*
                                 the Shem Ha Boreh

25)   Name: **NITAYAH (Nee-tay-YAH)**
       Meaning: *Yah is Extended/Inclined/Directed*
       Etimology: נטה = To be inclined, extended,
                             stretched, directed, bend down low,
                             deviate, turn aside.
                             יה = the self existent one

Gematria Sum: **74**
Position/Service: *One of the 72 Angels bearing*
                                 the Shem Ha Boreh

26)   Name: **HAHYAH (Hah-YAH)***

Position/Service: Governs the Order of Dominations,
Dimplomacy and Ambassadors.

27)   Name: **YIRATEL (Ye-raht-EL)**
       Meaning: *The Shooting forth/Instruction of EL*
       Etimology: ירת = To shoot, fire, throw, pour,
                             teach, instruct, direct, show, decide,
                             enjoin, command.
                             אל = Strength; The Strong One

Gematria Sum: **631**
Position/Service: Rules the Order of Dominations.

28) Name: **SEEHYAH (See-YAH)**
Meaning: *The Pinnacle/Excellency of YAH*
Etimology: **סיא** = Crest, pinnacle, record, summit, climax, peak, elevation, excellency.

יה = the self existent one

Gematria Sum: 326
Position/Service:Evoked to give long life and improve the health of those who invoke this name; Rules in the order of dominations.

29) Name: **REYIEL (Reh-Yi-El)**
Meaning: *The Sight/Vision/Appearance of El*
Etimology: **ראי** = Spectacle, Vision, Appearance Aspect

אל = Strength; The Strong One

Gematria Sum: 242
Position/Service: Serves in the Order of Dominations

30) Name: **OMAHYEL (Oh-mah-EL)**
Meaning: *El (Power) is the Foundation/Nation/People*
Etimology: **אומה** =*foundation, nation, people*

אל = Strength; The Strong One

Gematria Sum: 78
Position/Service: This Messenger multiplies races

31) Name: **LECABEL (Leh-Cahb-EL)**
Meaning: *To recieve/accept El (Strength)*
Etimology: **לקבל** = to receive; accept; take

אל = Strength; The Strong One

Gematria Sum: **163**
Position/Service: *Rules over vegetation/agriculture.*

32)   Name: **VASARYAH (Va-Sar-YAH)***

Gematria Sum: **515**
Position/Service: *The Order of Dominations*

33)   Name: **YEHUYAH (Yeh-hoo-YAH)**
       Meaning: *He is Yah*
       Etimology: יהו = He is
                    יה = the self existent one

Gematria Sum: **36**
Position/Service: The Order of Thrones or Powers; a guardian of princes.

34)   Name: **LEHADYAH (Leh-had-YAH)**
       Meaning: *Thank/Praise Yah*
       Etimology: להדה to reverberate, re-echo, echo, sound; to stretch out the hand (in thanks and/or praise)
                    יה = the self existent one

Gematria Sum: **54**
Position/Service: The Order of Thrones; a protector of princes.

35)   Name: **SHAVAKYAH (Shah-vahk-YAH)**
       Meaning: *Praise/Glorify Yah!*
       Etimology: שבח = Praise, glory, improvement, gain, betterment, excellence, to improve in value.
                    יה = the self existent one

Gematria Sum: **325**

Position/Service: One of the 72 Angels bearing the Shem Ha Boreh.

36)   Name: **MONADEL (Mo-nahd-EL)**
         Meaning: *El Casts Away/Expels*
         Etimology: מנד = Thrown/Cast Away

                       נדה = t o remove, cast out, expel, excommunicate, banish.

                       אל = Strength; The Strong One

Gematria Sum: **125**
Position/Service: *Unknown*

37)   Name: **ANIEL (Ah-nee-EL)**
         Meaning: *I am EL (Strength; Power)*
         Etimology: אני = I, I am

                       אל = Strength; The Strong One

Gematria Sum: **91**
Position/Service: *Guards the West Winds*

38)   Name: **HAAMYAH (Hah-aam-Yah)**
         Meaning: *The Kinsman/Relative/Nation of Yah*
         Etimology: עם = Kinsman, Relative; Nation, People, Folk, multitude, community, tribe, populace.

                       יה = the self existent one

Gematria Sum: **130**
Position/Service: A Messenger of the Order of Powers who guards over truth seekers & righteous organizations/communities.

39)   Name: **REYAEL (Rey-ah-EL)**
       Meaning: *A Friend is EL (Power/Strength)*
       Etimology: רעה = A friend, brother, companion, fellow, husband, lover, neighbor, associate.
                   רעה = idea, thought, meaning

Gematria Sum: **321**
Position/Service:The order of Dominations; rules over health and longevity, inspires respect for one's parents.

40)   Name: **YIYAZEL (Yee-yaz-EL)**
       Meaning: *El will Sprinkle/Shower Upon*
       Etimology: יז = To sprinkle
                   אל = Strength; The Strong One

Gematria Sum: **58**
Position/Service: *One of the 72 Angels bearing the Shem Ha Boreh.*

41)   Name: **HAHAHEL (Hah-Hah-El)**
       Meaning: *Alas! Behold! El (The Strong One)*
       Etimology: ההה = Woe! Alas! Ah! Behold!
                   אל = Strength; The Strong One

Gematria Sum: **46**
Position/Service: This Messenger exists within the Order of Virtues, protects Messiahs and Messianic representatives and followers.

42)   Name: **MICHAEL (Mee-Chay-EL)**
       Meaning: *One who is like unto EL; also El Pulps/Wounds/Impoverishes*
       Etimology: מי = who is
                   כ = as

אל = Strength; The Strong One

מכה =_ to pulp, macerate; impoverish; to blow, wound, plague, smote, beat, cause pestilence

Gematria Sum: **101**

Position/Service: *The Chief of Order of Virtues, Chief of Archangels, Prince of the Holy Presence, Messenger of Repentance, Righteousness, Mercy and Sanctification; Ruler of the fourth heaven (Zebul).*

43)   Name: **WEHLIYAH (Weh-lee-YAH)***
                (also Vevalyah)
      Meaning: *Yah is For Me*

Position/Service: *One of the 72 Angels bearing Shem Ha Boreh.*

44)   Name: **YELAYAH (Yeh-Lah-Yah)**
      Meaning: *Yah Will Enforce the Law*
      Etimology: לה = Law (Chaldean)
                 יה = the self existent one

Gematria Sum: **60**

Position/Service: *This Messenger serves in the Order of Virtues, protects magistrates and governs legal affairs/law suits.*

45)   Name: **SAALYAH (Saah- ahl-YAH)**
      Meaning: *Cure/Remedy of Yah*

      Etimology: סעל = Cure, Remedy
                 יה = the self existent one

Gematria Sum: **175**

Position/Service: *Governs the earth's vegetation.*

46)   Name: **ARIEL (Ah-ree-EL)**
      Meaning: *Lion/Brave One/Gatherer of EL*
      Etimology: Ahree (ירא) = Lion
                     Ahrah (הרא) = to gather, pluck, pick
                     אל = Strength; The Strong One

Gematria Sum: **242**
Position/Service: *Rules over water, one of the Seven*
Princes, Third   *Archon of the Wind.*

47)   Name: **ATSALYAH (Ah-Tsal-YAH)**
      Meaning: *Yah Delegates/Influences/Imparts*
      Etimology: Atsal **(אצל)** = To reserve, delegate,
                     impart, influence.
                     יה = the self existent one

Gematria Sum: **53**
Position/Service: A member of the Order of Virtues who
has rulership over Justice.

48)   Name: **MIHAEL (Mee-Ha-EL)**
      Meaning: *He Who is Like unto EL (The Strong*
                     One; Power/Strength)
      Etimology: **מי** = who, he who (is)
                     ה = the
                     אל = Strength; The Strong One

Gematria Sum: **86**
Position/Service: *One of the 72 Angels bearing the*
                     Shem Ha Boreh.

49)   Name: **VEHUEL (Veh-Hoo-EL)**
      Meaning: *And He is EL (Strength/Power)*

Etimology: ‎ו‎ = And

‎הוא‎ = He/It (is)

‎אל‎ = Strength; The Strong One

Gematria Sum: **48**

Position/Service: A member of the Order of Principalities

50) Name: **DANIEL (Dah-nee-EL)**

Meaning: *El Rules/Judges Me*

Etimology: ‎דנה‎ = To judge, punish, govern, rule, sentence, argue, contend

‎אל‎ = Strength; The Strong One

Gematria Sum: **95**

Position/Service: A member of the Order of Principalities who has authority over Representatives of the Law.

51) Name: **HAHAZIYAH (Ha-Hazi-YAH)**

Meaning: *The Vision/Dream/Perception of YAH*

Etimology: ‎הזה‎ = To Dream, visualize, percieve

‎חזיה‎ = Dream, Vision, Perception

‎יה‎ = the self existent one

Gematria Sum: **32**

Position/Service: *One of the 72 Angels bearing the Shem Ha Boreh.*

52) Name: **IMAMYAH (Ee-mam-YAH)**

Meaning: *Yah Obscures/Darkens*

Etimology: ‎עמם‎ = to dim; obscure

‎יה‎ = the self existent one

Gematria Sum: **165**
Position/Service: *A member of the Order of*
Principalities.

53) Name: **NANAEL (Nah-Nah-EL)**
    Meaning: *Behold EL (Strength/Power)*
    Etimology: נא = Please, Pray (would
    you), Behold
    אל = Strength; The Strong One

Gematria Sum: **53**
Position/Service: *A Member of the Order of*
Principalities who has dominion over the great sciences
and influences philosopher's and ecclesiastics.

54) Name: **NITAEL (Nee-tah-EL)**
    Meaning: *El is Directed/Extended/*
    Stretched Out
    Etimology: נטה = to be extended,
    stretched out, directed
    נטה = To stretch out, extend, be
    inclined to, to bend down low, turn
    aside, deviate
    אל = Strength; The Strong One

Gematria Sum: **90**
Position/Service: *A member of the Order of*
Principalities.

55) Name: **MEBAEL (Meh-Bah-EL)**

Position/Service: *Dominion over Morality/Spirituality*
and helps those desiring children.

56) Name: **POIEL (Poh-ee-EL)**
    Meaning: *Here is The Strong One; Revive, El!*
    Etimology: **פוע** = to breath into, blow, revive
    אל = Strength; The Strong One

Gematria Sum: **191**
Position/Service: A member of the order of Principalities who governs future blessings and philosophical teachings.

57) Name: **NAMAMYAH (Nah-mam-YAH)***

Position/Service: One of the 72 Angels bearing the Shem Ha Boreh.

58) Name: **YAHLIEL (YAH-Lee-EL)**
    Meaning: *Yah is Strength/Power (to me)*
    Etimology: **יה** = The Self Existing One
    לי = to me, unto me, for me, me
    אל = Strength; The Strong One

Gematria Sum: **86**
Position/Service: One of the 72 Angels bearing the Shem Ha Boreh.

59) Name: **HARAHEL (Har-ah-EL)**
    Meaning: *El (Strength/Power) is Revealed/Shown*
    Etimology: **הרה** = to be shown, revealed, demonstrated
    אל = Strength; The Strong One

Gematria Sum: **242**
Position & Service: Dominion over documentation & *stored information*

60)   Name: **MITZRAEL (Meetz-rah-EL)**
        Meaning: *El Binds/Borders/Subjects*
        Etimology: מצר = to bind, border, limit, subject
                       אל = Strength; The Strong One

Gematria Sum: **261**
Position/Service: *An 'Arch Angel' or Chief Messenger who induces obedience towards superiors.*

61)   Name: **UMABEL (Oo-mahb-EL)***

Position/Service: dominion over physics and astronomy

62)   Name: **YAHAHEL (YAH-ha-EL)**
        Meaning: *YAH is The Strength/Power/The Mighty One*
        Etimology: יה = The Self Existing One
                       ה = the
                       אל = Strength; The Strong One

Gematria Sum: **51**
Position/Service: Has dominion over philosophers/ truth seekers and all who seek to rise above carnality/the cares of the world.

63)   Name: **ANUEL (Anoo-EL)**
        Meaning: *Submit/Answer to El*
        Etimology: ענה = to answer, submit, hearken, hear, bear witness; to sing, respond, call out; to be humble, bowed down, oppressed, suffer

Gematria Sum: **157**
Position/Service: *One of the 72 Angels bearing the Shem Ha Boreh.*

64) Name: **MEHEKIEL (Meh-Heh-chay-EL)**

Position/Service: *One of the 72 Angels bearing the Shem Ha Boreh*

65) Name: **DAMABIYAH (Dah-Mahb-Yah)**

Position/Service: *A Messenger with dominion over Naval Construction*

66) Name: **MENIEL (Mee-nee-EL)**

Position/Service: *One of the 72 Angels bearing the Shem Ha Boreh.*

67) Name: **EHYAHEL (Eh-YAH-EL)**

Position/Service: *Rulership over Spiritual Sciences & longevity*

68) Name: **HABUYAH (Hah-Booh-Yah)**
Meaning: *Give Unto YAH*
Etimology: הב = to give
יה = the self existent one

Gematria Sum: **28**
Position/Service: *Dominion over agriculture & fruitfulness*

69) Name: **ROOAHEL (Roo-ah-EL)**
Meaning: *EL (Power) is Seen/Understood/Observed*
Etimology: רואה = to be seen

ראה = to look at, conceive, observe, understand, prefer, approve

אל = Strength; The Strong One

Gematria Sum: **237**

Position/Service: A Messenger who has power to find lost objects.

70)   Name: **YIBAMIYAH (Yee-Bah-Mee-YAH)**

Position/Service: One of the 72 Angels bearing the Shem Ha Boreh.

71)   Name: **HAYAHEL (Ha-YAH-EL)**
        Meaning: *Yah is EL (Strength/Power/The Strong One)*

        Etimology: יה = the self existent one

        אל = Strength; The Strong One

Gematria Sum: **51**
Position/Service: One of the 72 Messengers of the Zodiac

72)   Name: **MUMIYAH (Moo-mee-YAH)**
        Meaning: *Mutilation of Yah*
        Etimology: מום = mutilation, deformity, defect, blemish

        ממות = death, mortal disease; corpse

        יה = the self existent one

Gematria Sum: **101**
Position/Service: Dominion over health and longevity, science of physics and medicine/ healing

140

Bibliography for this Chapter

The Book of Angels, Gustav, Davidson

The Brown-Driver-Briggs, Hebrew and English Lexicon, F. Brown, S. Driver, C. Briggs

The Complete Hebrew-English Dictionary, R. Alcalay

* Asterik indicates meaning unknown

THE FOUR WORLDS

The consciousness of the majority of mankind is limited to the perception and understanding of one world, the tangible, material, physical, manifested world - the physical realm. However, ancient Hebraic cosmogony explains the existence of three other worlds beyond this one, and out of these worlds everything that was, that is, and that is to come, has its source and its essence in these realms.

The four worlds are as follows: The Atsilutic World of existence and emanation, the Briah World of Creation, the Yitzirah World of formation, and the Asiyah world of action and manifestation, (The continent of Asia was once called Asiyah, and encompassed the world as we know it today).

142

I. *Ha Olam Atsilut* (אצל)

<u>At-see-loot</u> = Aristocracy, nobility, emanation

<u>At-sal</u> = To delegate, emanate, influence, reserve, lay aside, set apart, impart

<u>At-seel</u> = noble, aristocracy

II. *Ha Olam Briah* (ברא)

<u>Briah</u> = Creation, making; world, cosmos

<u>Ba-rah</u> = To create, form, shape, make, produce

<u>Bahr</u> = Pure, clean, straightforward, pure in heart, sincere, frank, ingenuous

III. *Ha Olam Yitserah* (יצר)

<u>Yit-see-rah</u> = Creation, formation, production, deed, work, composition, creativeness, pottery.

<u>Yat-sar</u> = To create, manufacture, fashion, form, produce, contrive, devise

IV. *Ha Olam Asiyah* (עשה)

<u>Ah-see-yah</u> = An act, a doing, making, deed, performance

<u>Ahsah</u> = To make, do, work, labor, act, prepare, produce, yield, create, perform, accomplish, to cause, effect, execute, bring about, to appoint, keep, fulfill, to acquire, gain, to manage, to traverse, travel, spend, stay.

As the Tree of Life comes into existence, it emanates in the first World of Emanation, the Atsilutic World. Within

143

the Atsilutic World of Emanation, all the dynamics and laws are complete, except that nothing has happened, and nothing will happen unless there is movement in time and space. Neither does it yet exist, because the Atsilutic World is still at the stage of pure will and would have remained in this original state had not Yahweh El-Elyon willed the beginning of days called Shemitot in Hebrew. This divine presence was manifest in the highest world to the lowest substance, in time from Everlasting (El Olam in Hebrew) to the smallest manifestation of what is now, as it moves through the ages toward the end of the age. The tremendous motioning begins in the Atsilutic World and is generated by the laws of the Sefirot - the ten divine principles of Yahweh El-Elyon.

Isaiah speaks of the fourfold process of existence in the following words:

> *"Even everyone that is called by my Name;*
> *for I have created him for my glory, I have*
> *formed him: yea, I have made him."*
> Is. 43.7.

These four levels of creation: *1) Calling - Atsilut, 2) Creating - Briah, 3) Forming - Yitzirah, and 4) Making - Asiyah*, recur throughout the Kabbalah, the book of concealed mysteries of the scriptures. The four worlds exist within the Atsilutic World and correspond symbolically to the four letters of the most Holy Name of Yahweh, called the Tetragrammaton. The ten principles of existence are associated with the four elements of the lowest Sefirah (singular form of Sefiroth), Malkuth.

The first level is fire and is closest to the Crown, Keter, symbolic of pure will, the divine calling. The second level is associated with air and is symbolic of the intellect (spirit), it is the level of divine creation. The third level of water is symbolic of the emotions; it is the level of divine forming. The forth level associated with earth is the level of physical manifestation and is the level of divine making.

Each level contains the qualities and activities of the one above and as the motioning of existence descends further from the source, it is under more complex and defined laws.

Although the Atsilutic World is perfect within itself and with all existence, it must unfold itself in four stages, each a different world within itself. It is like the will to have the partner who is perfect for you; he or she has been conceived in principle and contains the germ of all the processes but yet has not manifested in physical form. The four levels of the Atsilutic World unfold themselves in four stages. Fire is conceived in the Atsilutic World of pure will, motioning forth into the second world of Briah, where air and spirit emerges. From Briah, a fluid world of formation motions forward into the third world of Yitzirah, which brings forth the world of solids, liquids, and gases - the Asiyah world (earth) in which the partner, the house, the child, the money, which you conceived of takes on a physical form. Each stage is governed by its own laws and incorporates the dynamics of the Atsilutic World.

The understanding of the relationship between the four worlds lies in the Hebrew scriptures of the Bible. "The divine calling by My Name," is the substance of Atsilut, and each Sefirah has attached to it one of the divine names of Yahweh El-Elyon. Kether, the crown, has the name Eheiyeh Asher Eheiyeh, `I Will Be What I Will to Be." The Sefirot of Wisdom (Kokmah) and Understanding (Benah), have been given the names Yah and Yahweh and are associated with the Merciful (Chased) and the Just (Din) aspects of the principle. (See Shield of David, Page

121). At Tiferet, which is the focus of the paths from these three Sefirot is Yahweh Elohim, the Almighty Creator, known by the composite name of YHWH Elohim. The rest of the Sefirot have divine names of their own; they are not a part of the creative aspects of His name but have attributes of their own in relation to Yahweh El-Elyon, the Most High Power. In the opening sentence of Genesis, "Bereshith Bara Elohim et Ha Shamayeem Ve Ha Aretz' translates figuratively as 'In principle Elohim created the heavens and the earth.' The word Elohim is plural; the creative process which is in the attributes of Yahweh's divine names, willed creation to be called forth.

In Hebraic Cosmogony, the first chapter of Genesis (Bereshith), speaks of the unfolding process of creation from an already existing world. All creation is called forth by Eheiyeh Asher Eheiyeh, I will be what I will to be, at Tiferet, the focal point of the Atsilutic Tree. Here, Elohim creates, forms, and makes from the three lowest levels of Atsilut, a new world - Briah. In Genesis, the world of Briah manifested within a period of seven days. This creation was a step by step unfolding of the Tree of Life, with each level associated to a set of Sefiroth until the last day of creation came to rest in the lowest Briah Sefirah, that of the Kingdom, (Malkuth), and completing the creation which 'was good.' The first chapter of Genesis, verse twenty seven, says in Hebrew "Vayibra Elohim et Ha Adam, "So Elohim *Created* Adam." In the second chapter, verse seven, it says "And Yahweh Elohim Vayitzer et Ha Adam," 'And Yahweh Elohim *Formed* Adam.'

Chapter two of Genesis expresses the formative aspect of the Sefirah called Olam Ha Yitzirah, the world of formation. Yitzirah is the realm of differentiation where the spirits of the Briatic realm undergo countless modification into individual types and forms. This world is known as the Garden of Eden, in which the androgynous Man created in Briah (Genesis 2.27) is differentiated into the distinctions of male and female.

The Asiyah world emerges out of the one above and is the world in which we, as Adam and Eve, have descended. It is the world of energy and matter, solids, liquids, and gases - the world in which we experience through our senses.

The Asiyah world is peopled by what is called in Hebrew, Tachutonim, those who dwell below, and refers to all the beings in the manifested world. The Elohim of the upper worlds, who dwell above, are not perceptible through the ordinary senses; these are the angels and archangels, or the 'fish and fowl' (Gen. 1.26), who swim in the waters of the Yitzirah world of formation and fly in the air in the Briatic World of Creation.

The inhabitants of these worlds play a part in existence and although we do not directly perceive their presence we are nevertheless affected by them, as natural rhythms, suggestive ideas, planetary cycles, epochs of history, human spiritual progress.

Also, within the creative universe, there is what is known in Hebrew as Kelippot, or the World of Shells. This concept recognizes the existence of demonic or destructive forces. Their task is to test goodness, and though they appear to be evil, they are in reality workers of Elohim as observed in the book of Job. Satan being the master deceiver and tester. These chaotic forces function to disrupt the balance of the universe at the level of the three lower worlds. The Sheddim (who have a strong influence over mankind) are demonic forces opposed to mankind, who use the testing ability of the Kelippot and seek to use it against man. However, Adam, the first Elohim Man, as well as others who have descended from him, possess free will and choice as to what they will be influenced by. As a human being, man has the power of manifesting both good and evil.

SHIELD OF DAVID

MIDDLE PILLAR
(Mild)

Macroprosopus or Vast Countenance

1. KETER - CROWN
Eheiyeh Asher Eheiyeh

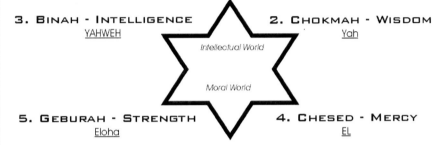

3. BINAH - INTELLIGENCE
YAHWEH

2. CHOKMAH - WISDOM
Yah

Intellectual World

Moral World

5. GEBURAH - STRENGTH
Eloha

4. CHESED - MERCY
EL

6. TIFERET - BEAUTY
Elohim
The King

Microprosopus or Lesser Countenance

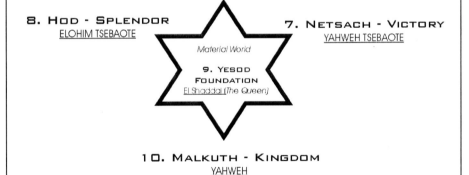

8. HOD - SPLENDOR
ELOHIM TSEBAOTE

7. NETSACH - VICTORY
YAHWEH TSEBAOTE

Material World

9. YESOD
FOUNDATION
El Shaddai (The Queen)

10. MALKUTH - KINGDOM
YAHWEH
Shekinah

THE SEFIROT (Tree of Life):

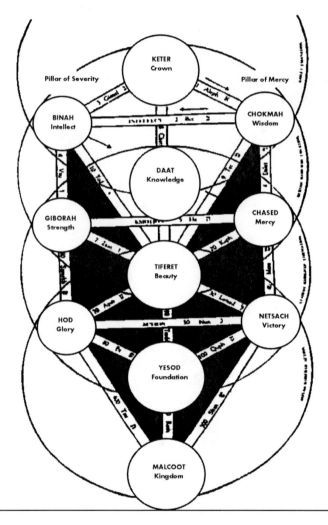

The diagram of the Sefirot or Divine Attributes was not published in full until the Middle Ages. There have been many variations but this is the version used by many Kabbalists today. Its structure contains all the laws that govern existence, because it reveals a universal process of balanced interaction between upper and lower, active (right) and passive (left) principles. The Divine influx can be traced in detail along the paths between the Sefirot (designed by the twenty two Hebrew Letters) and through the triads or three-cornered relationships that link them.

The four large circles show the levels within a single Tree which correspond to the four Worlds of Will, Intellect, Emotion and Action. Complex to the highest degree, the Sefirot Tree is nevertheless an image of Divine Unity. (The Tree of Life, its structure and dynamics).

The Likeness of a Man:

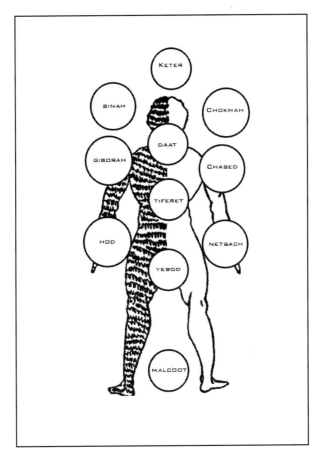

The likeness of a man (Ez. 1.26) was used by early mystics to describe the Divine Glory, (see above illustration). A primordial, Atsilutic man, created in the image of Yahweh Elohim, is the embodiment of the Sefirot, (The Tree of Life), the most perfect reflection of the Creator Himself. Atsilut, the Divine World of Emanation, is not Yahweh, but his garment of Light.

TRANSFORMATION OF THE MIND

With the application and transforming of your thoughts, by using the Sacred Names of Yahweh, nothing shall be impossible to you.

> *"Be ye not conformed to this age, but be ye*
> *transformed by the renewing of your mind,*
> *that ye may prove what is good and*
> *acceptable, and the perfect will of Yahweh."*
> *Romans 12.2.*

If we are to understand the faces of the Divine, we must begin to understand the face or the appearance of the light

152

body, that is seen when the Higher Intelligence or the Higher Mind speaks to you within your creative cycle of creation. When you have seen the face of the higher evolution and it speaks to you, even on the inner planes, you understand how the face of the Sons of Light, or of the Messengers of Light, is but a brain cell of Light that leads back into the Eternal Mind. The Eternal mind is all of the chemistry of Infinite Life Systems connected together through the greater creation of the mind-energy beyond celestial energy. We are told within the scriptures that there is a greater light threshold which is made out of the light PULSATION from every molecule of flesh, which can measure, resurrect, and reprogram all of the particles along with the Sacred names. Special breathing techniques are used to penetrate into the very consciousness of the names and to maintain a certain vibrational control over the psychochemical process. In a single intake, you absorb life, breath, spirit, nourishment, health, vigor and necessary conditioning to journey into eternity with special masters of the Father. The breathing passes through levels of Sound and Color, representing light energy at different levels of energy, whereby the participant experiences the flame growing brighter and brighter until he notices outlines of beings of light moving back and forth. The warmth and radiant tongues of flame unfold the garment of the Father unto us and become the efflorescence of His Love. The light grows until the flame within knows no fear but feels the excitement of His Divine Love. The Sacred Names also create the vehicle of Light which allows us to travel through the vibrations of the mind so that we can communicate with those who exist on thrones in the higher worlds of Yahweh, i.e. Celestial Beings, through transformation of thought, transformation of oneÆs magnetic field can be achieved, which allows this kind of communication to become possible.

Consider I Corinthians 15.51-56:

"Behold, I show you a mystery; we shall not all sleep (die), but we shall all be changed in a moment of a twinkling of an eye, at the last trump: for the trumpet shall sound and the dead shall be raised incorruptible, and we shall be changed. For this corruptible must put on incorruption, and this mortal must put on immortality. So when this corruptible shall have put on incorruption, and this mortal shall have put on immortality, then shall be brought to pass the saying that is written, `death is swallowed up in victory. Oh death, where is thy sting? Oh grave, where is thy victory?"

Corinthians is speaking of this in terms of a higher relativity, which is the releasing of the physical form. It is the releasing of the matter and the image and similitude which is in gravitational trapped light, which allows a new image of man to be constructed, to flow into the similitude of the luminaries who govern worlds beyond the earth's dimension. Let us now travel into and practice this mind of light by understanding how the Order of Melchizedek teaches us how to use thought to transform us into the Sons of Light.

THOUGHT

Thought is the supreme power within man and conscious thought is the power worker of miracles and the giver of every fine gift in your life. However, if the thought is occupied only with sensual and selfish desires, it then loses all power to attract the celestial elements from the Azilutic world of existence. You should continually direct your thoughts inward because within your own mind are the unseen forces which create everything in your environment. All doors are magically opened or tragically shut in the face of your thoughts. Whether you rejoice at the achievement of your heart felt desire in life or look to the past in sorrow at unfulfilled dreams is a result of your

thinking. In the expression of your thoughts, you should learn how to handle language just as expertly as a sculptor shapes his clay or an artist spreads his color upon the canvas, because your words carry within them your destiny.

Just as precise language has the ability to move people in purposeful directions, sloppy language can misdirect people. You must begin to use language that creates a sufficiently powerful rather than an unproductive and weak state for you. Precise language is decisive, careful, exact, well defined, truthful and leads one to results that are productive. In contrast, inaccurate, sloppy language is hasty, careless, incautious, loose, and results in effects that are enervating and non-productive. Some distortions in language can keep you from accomplishing goals in life and you should look for examples of these forms of expression in yourself and in others. An expression such as `I can't,' is neither true nor productive and you must not look for reasons why you can't but ask questions that will lead you back to power, such as "what would happen if I could." Thoughts such as these give you a list of possibilities and actions that you may not have seen before. When you claim depression for yourself - Oh, I feel so depressed, and ask yourself why you find yourself in this state, a long list of reasons will invade your thinking. But if you ask, `How am I depressed?' (exact, precise language), you begin to realize that there are certain things you do to create that state.

What do you picture in your mind? Do you picture the worst possible scene? What do you say to yourself? Do you speak in slow, low and sad tones - `I'm so depressed today. I feel terrible. I can't seem to do anything right,' and

then sigh a long, pitiful sigh. How do you sit? W_
Breathe? Depression doesn't just happen, you have to work at it! Once you become aware of how you put yourself in certain emotional states you can begin to create the opposite effect. The lesson to be learned in these examples is that no matter how dismal a situation may appear to you, you can question and examine your language and your actions so that it leads you away from the problem into the area of a powerful solution. You must have the courage to examine yourself.

What is yours in righteousness can be easily attained when the great spiritual laws combined with the power of the name of Yahweh and the twelve holy attributes is comprehended and put into practice in confidence and faith. Can you control your emotions so that through perfect peace they become a dynamo of spiritual power focused intensely on your target?

The instructions from the Order of Melchizedek are designed to help you develop that subtle power which makes your magnetic forces vibrate in every word you speak, in every image you visualize, and in every action you undertake.

All things exist in a state of constant vibration. Your human life is a state of vibration and when that vibration is stilled, your present life on this earth will end. Consider sound, for instance. Sound is a series of vibrations that registers in the human ear between the limits of forty and forty thousand vibrations per second. These figures set the limit of human hearing. When these vibrations reach the rate of four hundred thousand million, we see them in the form of light. All space is vibrating with light and sound, from the Atsilutic world, motioning itself through the Briah World, then to the Yitzirah World, and then sifting throughout the Asiyah world of manifestation. Normally our human senses are rigidly confined within narrow limitations. We are both deaf and blind to vaster rates of vibration, but when we learn to unify ourselves to these illimitable vibrations, we will have the ability to see and hear the things that exist in the Atsilutic world of existence, such as celestial beings.

You live entirely in your thinking. Every day the thoughts which you receive control your emotions and direct your reactions to the circumstances, the events, and the people in your life. Of course, you must recognize thoughts before you can act upon them. The rewards, the conditions, and the circumstances of your life will be measured by your thinking. The greatest and the most priceless gift you can receive is a transforming thought. You can only receive a thought. Thoughts come to you as gifts from the Atsilutic world of existence. It is true that a great many thoughts gathered through the five sense and often lodging in the mind, are negative, vain, silly, evil, and foolish, yet you alone have the ability to choose which thoughts you will express.

In destiny, you are given free will to choose that which is set before you. For every action there is an equal reaction; the universe is governed by these laws. For example, fire is neither negative or positive, but its use will determine the reaction it will cause. Man has the free will to choose how to use everything at his disposal. After changing your thought about Yahweh Elohim, the Almighty Creator, who wills all things into being, you must change your thought about yourself. You cannot, however, change what you are not conscious of. Therefore, you must meditate on the information given here until it becomes a part of your everyday thinking. Sit back and go into the silence. If you think about a thing long enough, there is an energy vibration that you pull to yourself and the thought becomes a part of you. Take time to reflect upon these ideas; they are energy, vibration, spirit. You cannot force a thought to be your own; it must be sealed in your soul with true acceptance.

Your thoughts create your character and your character is the real you. Picture yourself then, as the ideal you, which you really desire to be, and your mental picture will reflect itself in material reality. Intense desire brings opportunities to you. Possession is first mental. Action makes environment. Thinking without action is merely wishful day dreaming. You are forever affecting someone else - you bless people, or you make them worse. Your home life is either happy or miserable because of you or because of the negative thought vibration of someone else. Your own thought vibration creates every circumstances in your life and calls into being the results of every condition in your life. Your mental energy is the measure of your life; it is a personal product capable of infinite development when your thoughts are attuned to the infinite universal vibrations that are of Yahweh Elohim, the Almighty Creator. Yahoshua the Messiah stated that same great yet simple truth in these words,

> "If you abide in me (harmony of vibration),
> and my words abide in you (Yahweh's
> vibration in you), you shall ask what you
> will and it shall be done unto you." John
> 15.7.

Each thought exists as energy operating at the definite rate of vibration, and these rates of mental vibration differ greatly. Some thoughts have a very high rate, while others are very low. In the field of electricity there are two phases of energy current which are called positive and negative, likewise in the world about us we perceive these two great divisions of principle - day and night, light and darkness, good and evil. Negative thoughts are always destructive; they repel, they tear down, and they destroy. Positive thoughts are always creative; they attract, they build and they construct.

Referring to the ancient wisdom of the Bible, you will find approximately 741 separate references to the heart. Of these references the word heart is a figure of speech which can be properly interpreted to mean the mind. So, `Keep thy heart (mind) with all diligence, for out of it are the issues (results) of life." Proverbs 4.23. And again "As he thinketh in his heart (mind), so is he." Prov. 23.7.

Mind is synonymous with intellect, the center of perception and comprehension, the source of all mental and physical expression. It is the duty of the mind to know, to judge, to reason, and to understand. The ceaseless activities of your mind are devoted to perception, emotion, memory, and thought. There are many people who strongly desire to transform sickness into health, sorrow and frustration into success and peace, or trade limitation for total freedom but do not know how. Every day with the tool of thought, you are shaping what you choose, whether you are aware of it or not. With this tool, you bring forth from the Atsilutic world of existence, a thousand joys or a thousand sorrows.

Have you been the unconscious slave of circumstance? Perhaps unknowingly you have become the servant of your surroundings, or of self seeking people who have become human parasites. Maybe you have found yourself engaged in a struggle with 'wicked spirits in high places,' all diverting your efforts from accomplishment and success. Yielding yourself servant to the deceptive spiritual forces which many times manifest as inaccurate personal opinions, whims or ideas from others, is not for you and will not aid your transformation. Thought is a magnet which attracts to the thinker its own exact likeness, good or bad, positive or negative, health or sickness, poverty or riches, joy or sorrow. Thought creates that likeness unto material existence in all the things which make up the life of the thinker, therefore, as is your mind, so is your life, so are you.

Sickness, poverty, debt, troubles, misfortunes, and unwholesome environments are deceptive and destructive. Thought is energy and power and when you spend time thinking about these destructive conditions your very thinking and your fear gives reality, energy, and power to these dark enemies. *'Satan, the master deceiver is, but he is not, and these things that come from him are, but they are not.'* For countless ages man has thought reality into these great negations by his constant fear thoughts. Job began to understand the awful cost of fear when he cried out, *'The thing I greatly feared hath come upon me.'*

Your thoughts are seeds that blossom into fruit, so there is great danger in planting thought seeds of self pity, worry, doubt, fear, anger, hatred, jealousy, discouragement. These particular thoughts result in chronic or permanent failure and in physical suffering from one or more afflictions of the human system known as disease. The way to neutralize such thoughts is to boldly examine them and replace them

with well defined, productive thoughts. Thought seeds are a mighty power in your personal world. All mental activities change us and in changing us they change the world around us. Your thinking not only changes things outside yourself, but your mental activities also change your physical body, bringing about very real changes in your circulation, digestion, nerve and muscle tension and your breathing. You have probably often seen how clearly the faces of people around you are actually changed by joy, fear, love, etc. The features of almost all men and women reflect their emotions very plainly. When you learn to read the features of people, you are learning to read people spiritually. Each line upon your face, the smile or the frown, the magnetic gaze or that uncertain look in your eyes, all reveal your own real habit patterns of mind, your secret thought made visible.

The first achievement, the first victory is to entirely sever yourself from the mistaken concepts and the base ideas of unthinking people who surround you. This is true because the understanding of the great mass of people is usually undeveloped. The ability to think for yourself, this mental separation from the crowd, is one of the great reasons why you succeed. Remember, mental independence and personal individuality help you to magnify your vision and insure you the possibility of attaining your greatest desire. You will succeed when it doesn't matter to you if a million or ten million people try to teach outmoded and worn-out theories of life around you, nor does it matter to you what robes of authority they assume. You will succeed in exact degree as you use this ability to think for yourself, to free yourself from the hindering influence of common place ideas, narrow concepts, and lack of mental vision.

It is often true that those closest to you can often quite unconsciously be the greatest foes to your achievement. This was the thought Yahoshua expressed in the words, *'and a man's foes shall be they of his own household,'* Matt. 10.36. These relatives and close associates feel that they have always known you and they will claim that your new ideas are foolish, or through unconscious envy they may ridicule your advanced vision. Some may actually resent the fact that you are attracting the finer things in life through your vision as reflecting upon their own inferiority. In learning to think for yourself, you should also realize that silence is golden, regarding your spiritual work. This is emphasized to impress upon you that there are few to whom you can safely reveal your inner thoughts and your heart's desire.

You alone decide whether you will live life in a little way or whether you will live life graciously and richly; magnify your vision and you magnify your life. When you choose the spiritual life you will discover that it requires no more labor or effort to live on a broad scale that it does on a small one. The only difference between the successful corner grocer and the man who directs a successful and thriving chain of supermarkets is the size of mental picturing each man habitually holds.

You may find that you know or have known some man or woman (maybe even yourself) whose lack of success puzzled you because they seemed to have a mind filled with wonderful dreams, visions, and insights. Maybe this person has had an extensive education, has traveled and has a wealth of information to share, yet this person remains a mediocre failure. Why? What is it that makes one person succeed and another fail miserably? The key that opens doors to success is the courage to act upon the guidance that comes to you. You must have perfect confidence in that strong guiding mental impression which often pops up suddenly from the depths of your being and says, *'you can do it! Get busy and I'll show you how! I'll lead the way if you'll just listen, obey and act.'*

We should watch for and not neglect that guiding light that flashes across the mind from within. We limit our self expression and are ashamed of the divine ideas that are within us because we see the false security of conformity. It is the belief of the masses that conformity is virtue while non-conformity is sin. Man has a stake in the past, and for him the past is more important because it is established, grounded. Man does not live in the present but seeks repose in the dead past. So for you to bring new, vibrant and creative thought to his consciousness, is to upset that which is already established. For example, if he is told that the way he has been praying is wrong, and he has been praying that way for forty years (still waiting for results) there is much stake in this. To believe this is to believe that for forty years his prayers have been useless. He will fight; he will defend. Man is basically timid and dares not to think for himself. He would rather quote some ancient sage or repeat some time worn doctrine rather than speak those powerful words, I think. For thousands of years, man has been doing certain things, and when a new thought emerges, coming in the form of an individual, it melts, it uproots, it confuses, and it shakes all that was thought to be significant. 'Man-made traditions are a traitor to the truth' - an accomplice in the murder of spontaneous thinking.

164

Society is in conspiracy against the independence and determination of its members.

The masses of humanity remain lifeless figures carved of stone as far as thinking is concerned. They have eyes but do not see, ears but do not hear, brains but do not understand. They have no mind of their own. For centuries they have been conditioned, hypnotized, and brainwashed. So only a very few people who are really seekers of truth will be ready to go through the turmoil that independent thinking causes. Lies can be comfortable and convenient but they lead to spiritual death. Truth, in the beginning is very inconvenient and uncomfortable, but in the end it is the ultimate blessing which leads to freedom. People like freedom, but they are fearful of it. When freedom is not there, they think about it, they fantasize about it, but when the opportunity for freedom comes, they become afraid because freedom brings with it much more than great adventures - but responsibility. It can bring insecurity, danger and even death.

Only in solitude will you be able to know the truth, and when you find truth, you must be bold enough, courageous enough to speak it. The true test of conviction which reveals greatness of character, is the ability to maintain your independence of thought in the midst of the crowd. In order to break the bonds of the mass mind you must begin to test, inquire and to question. Question totally and intensely so that it will become a sword in your hand, cutting away all the accumulated refuse from eons ago. One who questions and searches to the very end will find the answer. Those who go on believing without questioning remain dull. So question and meditate, be silent and listen with an active ear. Silence needs courage as does doubt, for silence is like an abyss - no tradition to hold on to, no established ideas to lean on, and no mass mind to find security in. In the beginning you may experience fear because of the total sense of aloneness you feel; you have nothing to hold onto but yourself. But slowly, almost imperceptibly, from out of the emptiness comes a vastness of hidden treasures, a plethora of impassioned thoughts and a nourishing sense that you alone are enough. Ask yourself whether what you are thinking is coming from the Creator or from someone else. Is it borrowed experience or is it your own - arrived through questioning and listening to the intuitive truth inside of you with an active ear. Put aside all man made knowledge, all hypotheses, all voices from the crowd; discover the voice of truth within and follow it without fear. Insist on being your true self, going beyond the crowd, beyond the clear-cut, formulated, limited scope of the society, because beyond it is the vastness of Elohim, the Almighty Creator. Follow your lonely path. Be alone and exist as if you are the center of the world. At first you will feel the inner pain and suffering but when the transformation starts, you will begin to see the inner riches and treasures that exist within you, not the treasures that are spread all around you. Once you do this, you will find that the Creator will rush toward you. Love yourself enough to search for and express what is original and pure in you. Trust your nature and accept yourself as you are, for with acceptance comes a natural transformation.

Strong habits of thought directed toward the accomplishment of great goals have made men master over heredity, over environment and have redeemed them of sickness and weakness of all kinds. It is the thinker who always changes the world around him or her. When you realize fully the truth that your thoughts and your emotion bring about causes and effects in your life just as exact and infallible as chemical reactions, then you can understand yourself and those around you scientifically. You will see man as a self determined being - thought born, thought inspired, thought destroyed or thought empowered.

Throughout the ages the masters of all fields have started with unbounded faith in their inner voice, with an original idea and a positive mental attitude. The difference between those who succeed and those who succumb to negative influences and fail, is self-reliance, faith in a positive guiding thought and courage in following their deep seated voice. Spirit works its miracles in your life by the power of faith. Faith is a firm confidence, a vivid expectation, based upon your knowledge that you are attuned to the Atsilutic world of existence, where the substance of all material exists in a formless state. Remember, it is your strong, unwavering attention which draws invisible power to your silent work. Your unceasing attention creates the realization in your mind that you are drawing upon the power of a boundless reservoir of substance. Your source is Yahweh Elohim El-Elyon, the Almighty Creator, and the Most High Power of Powers.

When the highest state of spiritual development is attained, the spirit, endowed with the highest spiritual activity of the Neshamah (the soul), attracts to itself, Truth. This truth perceives and knows the conditions, causes, and effects of all external and internal natural and holy things. By this process, Man - though existing in a limited bodily form - may know all that exists in the internal and external world, and see all things, not merely things which are, but also those things which have been, as well as those things which will be. With this high spiritual activity of the soul comes the power to change things with the power of the word. At this stage your words will carry the full and magnetic power of your thoughts. When you talk, your words will vibrate with creative power for you have attuned your mind with the Power of Powers:

"The fear of Yahweh is the Beginning of Wisdom, but fools despise wise instruction." Pr. 1.7

IMAGING POWER IN THE SILENCE: ACHIEVING YOUR CHIEF DESIRE

The purpose of this chapter is to bring you more fully the truth that not only are you endowed with latent talents, faculties, and forces that know no bounds of possibility, but that working with you and at your conscious command is Yahweh El-Elyon, the Most High Power. This force is an invisible ocean of power that touches your life in every way once you admit this truth into your thinking, and from which you can draw personal power that will build reality into the vision of your heart's desire. The vision referred to is your mental picture of your heart's desire, the picture which reflects that which you most greatly long for, which you most deeply desire, and which represents life's highest attainment to you. Within your reach is this vast reservoir of power awaiting only your conscious demand to transform your life. Creative power from the Atsilutic world of existence is at this moment surging through your mind, through your body, and through the depths of your soul, seeking to establish in your daily life the reality of your mental picture, your cherished vision.

There is a tremendous difference between sound, practical, effective imaging and fruitless daydreaming. Constructive imaging or effective mind pictures are always directed towards actually changing outside conditions, towards bettering your objective world, and endeavoring to create new life for yourself. Whenever one visualizes, images, or formulates mind pictures that are not definitely directed toward some specific objective, then he/she is simply daydreaming. It is true, however, that desires, which begin as mere day dreams, can - if faithfully continued - manifest as reality in the Asiyah world of manifestation.

Within every man and woman there are two definite and very distinct urges or mental trends. First, there is what is called the regressive urge, which is strong and also very subtle, usually so hidden that we are sometimes totally unconscious of it. It works to pull us back from true effort and from action. This is in reality a covert desire to escape reality. Regression mentally recedes towards childhood's dream word of protection. The general trend of most humans today is regressive. As this regressive mind or desire goes on toward dominant day dreaming, it becomes more and more universal among the people of the earth.

This day dreaming is nothing more than the imaginary realization of the longings of men for seeming superiority, for glory, or for imaginary grandeur *easily* acquired. Because this regressive day dreaming is most harmful to your upward progress, we must warn you against the dangers of this mental attitude. The other and more conscious urge you will recognize within yourself is the urge to action, to self expression, to meet and master your world, and to enjoy your destiny.

> *"Every good gift and every perfect gift is*
> *from above and cometh down from the*
> *Father of Lights, with whom is no variables,*
> *neither shadow of turning." James 1.17.*

In the invisible world all around you vibrate forces, energies, and powers which as you progress through every higher grades of spiritual growth, you will learn to harness and use. Learn from the great ones of the world. Over and over according to history they have risked their fortunes, their reputations and often all they had, on a decision seemingly made on the spur of the moment and always they have greatly succeeded. What did they put their faith in? To whose voice were they listening? Without a doubt, to Yahweh El-Elyon, the Most High Power within them. Supreme success always follows this course of action.

Yahweh El-Elyon, the Most High Power, is the power that has created a million spheres endlessly whirling in space; this power can create matter in the thinking of the brain, out of the invisible, and then set that matter into ageless motion either as a world or as a pebble. This is the intelligent creative power of Yahweh Elohim, the Almighty Creator, which you draw unto yourself in each of your concentration periods. This power is available at any hour in any place wherever and whenever you follow the laws of concentration.

Your heart's desire, which vibrates constantly and strongly, will irresistibly attract into your environment from the Azilutic world of existence, each and every element necessary to fulfill that desire; you will notice a change in your life day by day as you faithfully use your mind to focus on this greatest of powers. Remember, this fulfillment is a continuing process; this is not a fulfillment which is limited to one desire, but through this power which you are drawing from the universe, desire after desire is accomplished for you day after day, week after week, year after year, because vibration never dies. What you must keep uppermost in mind, though, is that your desire, your life plan, all carry unexpressed energies and powerful drives which can be scattered to the four winds of heaven if you tell others all about them. By keeping your own counsel, by keeping silent about your work, your plans, and your progress, you will easily avoid negative influences from others. These influences may come from friends or even close relatives, because the common mistake your daily associates usually make is in judging your future capabilities by your past lack of success or from their own lack of success. There is a saying, *'Never share your dreams with those who have not accomplished their own.'* Remember, when none around you know anything about what you are working for or how you are bringing these accomplishments into manifestation in your life, you do not have to overcome their belief in how it can't be done. Cherish your vision in the silence; conserve your energies for your transformation, for your mental exercises, and for your receptive periods of aloneness with the

Almighty Creator. After you have achieved, then you can reveal the secret to your success.

Consider the following: You have a great, definite purpose in life; you have chosen to build reality into your heart's desire. To this end you are constantly, continuously visualizing. In doing this, you are painting a picture upon the inner planes of your own consciousness and calling forth your reality from the Azilutic world of existence. Sooner or later this inner picture of yours, sharply drawn, clearly defined, and fully developed, if discussed with others will only tend to scatter and dissolve the results of your visualizing. If you feel a desire to discuss your picture, let it be with someone who you know will wholeheartedly support you.

> *"But thou, when thou prayest, enter into the*
> *closet (alone) and when thou has shut the*
> *door, pray to thy Father, which is in secret*
> *(in the invisible, in the silence) and thy*
> *Father which seeth in secret, shall reward*
> *thee openly. Matt 6.8.*

You must first contact this inner voice if you want that voice to guide you. Each and everyone of your exercises and periods in the silence is a step toward contacting that inner guidance. Tuning into this contact is not always easy. The more you rely upon and follow this inner gift, the faster it develops.

When you are imaging in the silence of Yahweh, you are calling all things into being for yourself here and now. The process is simple, but tremendous in its' importance. So important that you must thoroughly understand it. The danger being that some may miss the significance and value of this vital truth by a hasty or superficial glance and go mentally roaming in the search for some strange system, some magic formula or some peculiar and complex philosophy which will transform their lives without any understanding at all on their part. These are the dreamers, not the doers. Drifters can never be creators.

"Be still and know that I am Yahweh," is the command of the Almighty, through the words of King David. (Psalms 46.10).

In other words, relax, cease to strain in mind, body or soul. With perfect confidence, with faith, don't hope, don't guess, don't struggle-*know*. Each and every thing in your life is the materialization of imaging you have done, either knowingly or unknowingly in your own mind. Every good thing which you desire today, already exists dormant in the realm of your own thought world. Each of these good things can be awakened and materialized into being for you by the correct method of imaging, accompanied by desire, directed by faith. Every minute of your life you are using your imaging power. If you are sick, if you are failing, if you are unhappy, or if you are poor in earthly possessions, then you have simply been pulling the wrong thought pictures from the Atsilut world of existence.

Today we live in the strangest, perhaps most terrifying time of all history. Before us and all around us are manifestations of violence, pain, and destruction - a war torn world. However, amid it all the imaging power that is ours to use opens the doors of the heavens to us. Life never seemed less certain than now, but you have the power to change your life. If you are weak, life becomes a burden, so dare to be strong. Don't build obstacles across your path of destiny in life. Some people mentally image age as a limitation, but there are no deadlines to what you can accomplish except in your own mind. All to often, we say we cannot achieve because some government, person, place or economic condition hinders us. Be aware of what you image, for eventually you will get it. As the scripture warns us, '*To whom ye yield yourselves servants to obey, his servants ye are.*' Just as with nations, if you do not choose your own road, some cunning and cruel dictator will force you to travel his road, and you will find it a rough road and the going hard. The conditions which make up your life today are the direct result of your own imaging. If you are happy and successful, then it is because you have purposely imaged these qualities. You are the product of the desire which controls your imaging. You are then your own master, whether for good or for ill, for upon you depends the choice of the controlling desire which through your own imaging molds for you a life of health, joy, and success or one of sickness, misery, and failure.

Your thought image is the most important thing in the world to you. Make your mental picture distinct, make it wonderful to yourself, pour your emotions into it. By the depths of your own feeling you will make that image intense, vital, alive and *real*. The material world is built out of the world of dreams coming from the Atsilutic world of existence.

Take care to control your vision and focus upon your inner voice; listen with your heart, listen with your mind, listen with your soul. With each passing night, that inner voice will speak to you more clearly, more firmly, and more distinctly. Your triumph will come when after a few months you can rely upon that inner voice absolutely. Dismiss undesirable forms which may try to intrude upon your vision. In this work remember, you are in the presence of power. You must persist. Suppose that you started to play a musical instrument........ If you desired to reach a level of perfection, wouldn't you practice playing the instrument until you reached your goal?

Whenever and wherever possible, your period of concentration should be at night. There is not only a very deep psychological principle involved in choosing the hours of darkness for entering your period in the silence, but there is also a spiritual principle involved. According to the wisdom of the Bible, Yahweh El-Elyon, the Most High Power, is recorded as being closest to man in the manifestations of power during or in darkness. For Genesis 1.2 tells us that *"Darkness was upon the face of the deep. And the spirit of Yahweh moved upon the face of the waters."* Yahweh Elohim, the Almighty Creator, speaks often amid darkness,

> *"These words Elohim spoke unto all your*
> *assembly in the mount out of the midst of*
> *fire, of the cloud and out of the thick*
> *darkness." Deut. 5.22.*

The spiritual law of the universe still reveals secrets and gives power to Man at night, just as in the olden times:

> *"Then was the secret revealed unto Daniel*
> *in a night vision. Then Daniel blessed the*
> *Elohim of heaven." Daniel 2.19.*

Turning to the New Covenant, we find that darkness and night surround many manifestations of power. For instance, ". . . *in the fourth watch of the night, Yahoshua went unto them, walking on the sea." Matt. 14.25.* Let us not forget that woman was the last friend at the hanging of the Messiah and the first human to see Him risen in the last hours of the night:

"The first day of the week cometh Mary Magdelene early, when it was yet dark, unto the sepulcher." John 20.1.

Daylight is often disintegrating and confusing; night vibrates with calm silence and Yahweh El-Elyon, the Most High Power.

There is an inner power, silent and flowing ceaselessly throughout the universe. In concentration and meditation, this silence is tapped. The power is everywhere, outside and within matter; it is always present and everlasting. This is the light and source of your life. Use it well - that is, powerfully, carefully and confidently.

In your concentrated use of aphorisms, add life to each one by visualizing precise, colorful pictures of what you want to manifest in your life. The unseen power of Elohim, the Almighty Creator surrounds you like an ocean and by your repetition of certain powerful thoughts you are drawing into the depths of your being, power to work for you.

The Power of Thought:

"Yahweh Yireh El Shaddai, (All Sufficient Provider, Nourisher, Sustainer) is the supplier of my every need."

"I Trust in Yahweh with all my heart; and I will not lean to my own understanding."

PERSONAL POWER

Every being has a definite vocation and this vocation is the light which illuminates his life. When you disregard your vocation you become as a unlit lamp.

> *"For the Kingdom of Heaven is as a man traveling into a far country, who called his own servants, and delivered unto them his goods. And unto one he gave five talents, to another two; and to another one; to every man according to his several ability; and straightway took his journey. Then he that had received the five talents went and traded with the same, and made them other five talents. And likewise he that had received two, he also gained another two. But he that had received one went and*

dug in the earth, and hid his master's money. After a long time, the master of those servants cometh and reckoneth with them. And so he that had received five talents came and brought other five talents, saying, Sir, thou deliveredst unto me five talents; behold, I have gained beside them five talents more. His master said unto him, Well done, thou good and faithful servant: thou has been faithful over a few things I will make thee ruler over many things: enter thou into the joy of thy master. He also that had received two talents came and said, Sir, thou deliveredst unto me two talents: I have gained two other talents beside them. His master said unto him, Well done, good and faithful servant; thou hast been faithful over a few things, I will make thee ruler over many things: enter thou into the joy of thy master. Then he which had the one talent came and said, Sir, I knew thee that thou art a hard man, reaping where thou has not sown, and gathering where thou has not strewed: And I was afraid and went and hid thy talent in the earth: lo, there thou hast what is thine. His master answered and said unto him, Thou wicked and slothful servant, thou knewest that I reap where I sowed not, and gathered where I have not strewed: Thou oughtest therefore to have put my money to the exchangers, and then at my coming I should have received mine own with interest. Take therefore the talent from him, and give it unto him which has ten talents. For to everyone that hath shall be given, and he shall have abundance: but from him that hath not shall be taken away even that which he hath. And cast ye the unprofitable servant into outer darkness: there shall be weeping and gnashing of teeth." Matt. 25.14-30.

No matter what your position in life has been, no matter what your age may be, no matter what sickness you have claimed, no matter whether you are wealthy or have known poverty, just as surely as you follow the spiritual laws of the universe, you are an expanding soul. Just as with a radio, where there is one control knob by which you can tune into almost any broadcasting station, so with your thought radio, there is a control button by which you can almost as instantly contact and tune into the tremendous power of Yahweh El-Elyon, the Most High Power through mental acceptance. When you realize and have total faith in this truth, you will walk straight into the path of light. No longer will you stumble along in darkness, not knowing which way to turn, afraid to make a move, but you will walk with confidence and faith, with wide eyes, head erect and shoulders straight because you know exactly where you are going and you know exactly what to expect.

With this realization, you will no longer be content with any small manifestation of this power, but you will seek the greater things in life and know that with the proper approach you can attain a destiny rich in possibilities, a life radiant and glorious. There are no limitations when you walk in light. When you become conscious of the illimitable power everywhere around you and begin to command and direct it through your personal awareness of it, you can at any moment mentally build a world of your own which far exceeds the small, limited, and fearful world of the masses. Power from everywhere around you to build your new world is your heritage and birthright, but you must consciously claim that power.

Like the tides of the ocean, growth throughout all nature appears in cycles of progression where we see periods of seeming loss or decline. Growth is a series of periods of activity and periods of apparent inactivity. You will find this same changeless law governing your growth. You will experience times when it seems that you are in a decline. However, this inaction, this lack of progress is only apparent. During these times of apparent inaction, when you seem to be making little or no progress, you must beware of discouragement. Know that as long as you are working toward your transformation, on a deeper level a great change is taking place.

Your supreme destiny is in spiritual consciousness, which when developed, links your life with Yahweh Elohim, the Almighty Creator, who speaks to you from every natural law, who electrifies every particle of matter - the power behind all things. Use this magnetism which is all around you this very moment - that is its purpose. Complete mastery will be yours and your heart's desire will rapidly materialize into reality when you consciously absorb and use this magnetism or vital power which pervades all the atmosphere which surrounds this earth. By consciously using this vital power which is just as near to you as the air you breathe, you will be able to recreate the tissues of your body and to so fortify yourself against disease, that you will live in abounding health; sickness will pass you by untouched.

You are so great a soul that you have the power to choose your own level upon the scale of life and in choosing that level you have, of course, chosen the environment, the conditions, the circumstances and the people of that particular level.

Personal power and magnetic vibration are very closely related, in fact one depends on the other. If your magnetic vibrations are at a low ebb, your personal attracting power diminishes and weakens. When your personal power no longer attracts people of your kind and is not strong enough to repulse people who are negative, your magnetic power must be stepped up. This can be done by being in constant control of your thoughts. You must rule your thinking. Magnetic vibration, the source of your personal power, is a mental ray current directly ruled by your own thought. You can do and you can be what you think you can, so the greater the thought, naturally the greater the destiny.

When you think of yourself, do not think of that part of you that appears on the surface. That part is the smaller part and the lesser should not be pictured in the mind. Think of your larger self, the immense self that is limitless, both in power and in possibilities. Follow the vision of your own soul. Be true to your ideals, no matter what may be happening at the present, then things will take a turn and the very things you wanted to happen will happen. The ideal has a positive drawing power toward the higher, the greater, and the superior. Whoever constantly gives his attention to the ideal, will steadily reach it. Expect every change to lead you to something better and it will. As your faith, so shall it be.

The greater work of soul growth is a continuous work and cannot be completed in any brief period of time any more than your academic education was completed in your first week of school. Each desired thought is a vibration, but these thoughts are influenced by your mental conceptions and are confined or released by your mental understanding. *"Wisdom is the principle thing,"* said King Solomon, *"Therefore, get wisdom and with all thy getting, get understanding."* Those who have only little understanding can have only narrow conceptions of life, and of the Almighty Creator who wills all things to be.

In all the universe, there is no such thing as getting something for nothing. Under the Levitical Law spoken of in the he Bible, one tenth of all increase of crops, flocks, or money belonged to and was paid to Elohim:

> *"And all the tithe (tenth) of the land,*
> *whether of the seed of the land, or of the*
> *fruit of the tree, is Elohim's; it is holy unto*
> *Yahweh. And concerning the tithe of the*
> *herd, or of the flock, even of whatsoever*
> *passeth under the rod, the tenth shall be*
>
> *holy unto Elohim." Lev. 27.30-32.*

That is still the eternal law; you must give before you can receive. Before you can expect to reap a harvest, you must sow the seed, and just lending some seed will not do at all, you must actually give it without the least thought of ever getting it back. Unless your seed money of love and of labor is given freely and fully, you will get nothing in return, *'But if it die, it beareth much fruit.'* This is to say, that it must be dead to you, you have simply given it with no hope of recall or return of the seed. But once you comply with the eternal law, you can confidently expect a rich abundant harvest. The power of Yahweh El-Elyon, the Most High Power, demonstrates through you, but you cannot imprison this divine power within the walls of your own little personal world. You must give out, express, live and reflect this power in everything you do, day to day. To attract and receive the treasures in life which you greatly desire requires that you give generously and freely of whatever you now have. Whatever talent you now have, don't hide it; get busy giving it as seed for the harvest.

Don't dam up the channels of supply by hoarding what you have been blessed with, because then you completely stop the flow of Yahweh's blessings into your life.

Never imagine yourself to be an isolated unit in the universe or in the world of things around you. Step by step, your transformation leads you higher and higher as your mind stretches outwards and your soul develops. As your mental vision becomes clearer and clearer, then more and more you will be able to realize the unity and oneness between yourself and the Most High Power; you will consciously recognize that power as the source of all things in your life. Life throughout the universe is forever in action. Your life, like a swinging pendulum, is action and reaction. Back of the action and the reaction in your life, is your real self - I WILL BE WHAT I WILL TO BE.

The Body is an Electro-chemical Plant:

The human body is composed of several bodies. The physical body is material and tangible; the others are composed of much more subtle substances or vibrations with a shape identical to that of the physical body, and these bodies are present as long as the person lives.

The etheric or astral formative, created, emanated bodies can be called into manifestation in the physical body by the level of thought that is put forth. All space is electrically vibrating with sound. Throughout interstellar space speeds electrical waves of vibration tremendously beyond our limited hearing of forty thousand vibrations per second. Our human senses are rigidly confined within narrow limits. We are both deaf and blind to these vaster rates of electrical vibrations. When they reach the astounding rate of four hundred thousand million, we see them in the form of light. There is boundless creative opportunity and untold powers in Yahweh El-Elyon's, the Most High Power's, great universe for the use of that hitherto unknown electrical vibration of your invisible self, the mind, which we call thought.

The body is an electrochemical plant literally in motion throughout the day and night and relaxation is essential to vitality and to life itself.

All that exists in the human body motions from the laws of polarity; every atom, every cell in the entire system possesses two poles: electric and magnetic or positive and negative. Poles are the extreme point of an axis with opposite physical qualities. The ability to exist depends upon forces of interaction between the two terminal points.

The human system functions in accordance with the laws of polarity in which the key points are the head and the feet. They constitute the poles between which the ten separate energy currents circulate - five in each half of the body between the head, the five toes and the five fingers. The head is the crown point where the electrochemical polarity law of thought exists,

> *"For as he thinketh in his heart (mind) so is he." Prov. 23.7.*

> *"So keep thy heart (mind) with all diligence, for out of it are the issues of life." Prov. 4.23.*

> *"Thou will keep him in perfect peace whose mind is stayed on thee: because he trusted in thee; Trust ye in Yahweh forever, for- Yahweh is the Rock of Ages (Yahweh El- Olam)." Is. 26.3-4.*

It is very important that you do not put your hand out to people to suddenly, for every one carries a vibration, positive or negative, which can be transmitted from one person to another.

> *"Lay hands suddenly on no man, neither be partaker of other men's sin (falling short); keep thyself pure." II Tim. 5.22.*

Levitical Sign of Blessing of The Shield of David:

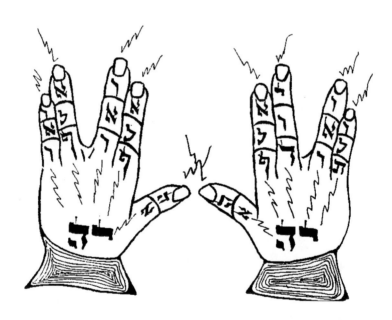

HAND EXERCISES AND MEDITATION

FIRE

HEALING

AIR

WATER

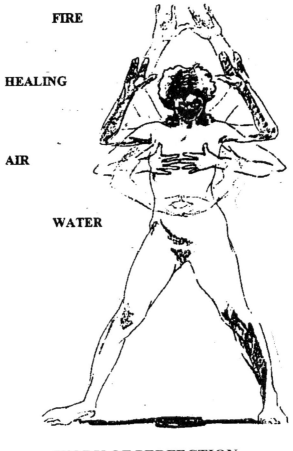

WORK OF PERFECTION

In these meditations both hands are held in the same signs in the positions shown in the above illustration.

Above the head, the sign of fire is made; on the breast, the sign of air is made, in the area below the navel, the sign of water is made; and in front of the forehead, over the third eye, the sign of healing is made.

HOLDING HAND OF POWER

WORD OF POWER: YAHWEH EL ELYON

Each hand sign relates to a specific vibration as the 'Words of Power' are repeated during the exercises. The Words of Power are the Holy Name of Yahweh coupled with any of his infallible Divine Attributes. These words can be chanted in song or spoken with the soft hum of the inner voice.

The most universal of all Words of Power is 'Amen,' which means 'faithful,' or 'So be it.' A prayer or meditation without 'Amen' at the end has no power. 'Amen' – or an affirmation of your faith – is the working tool of Yahweh.

The vibration of the Words of Power generate first from you, emanating first from the mind through the vocal chords which transfer the energy t to the hands, the spine, and throughout the whole body. Also, in your 'calling' upon the Holy Name(s) of Yahweh, you are also invoking and inviting His Divine Presence to enter your temple. Therefore, your hands (when held in the hand positions wherein the fingers are projected upward towards the heavens, see page 153-155) become a receptor of the greater Universal Spiritual Energy and Life Force, allowing you to subsequently become a transmitter of this Divine Energy (i.e. for healing, blessing, prayer, etc.)

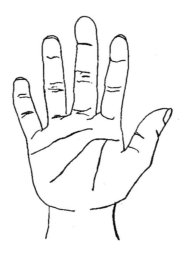

SIGN OF AIR

(+) WORD OF POWER*

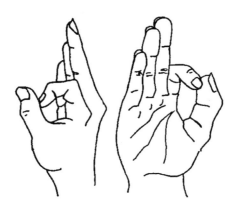

SIGN OF WATER

(+) WORD OF POWER*

UNIVERSAL SIGN OF FIRE

(+) WORD OF POWER*

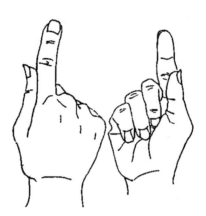

BASIC SIGN OF FIRE

(+) WORD OF POWER*

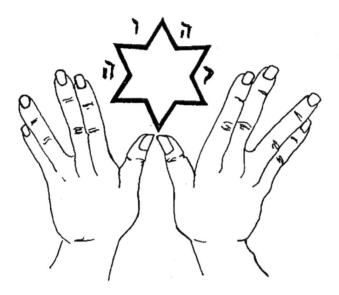

LEVITICAL BLESSINGS AND HEALINGS

WORD OF POWER: YAHWEH ROPHEH

The exercises of the hands have the names of the ancient elements of Fire, Water and Air.

The Signs by the hands and with the Words of Power are contemplated during the exercises.

Have you ever touched something or somebody and got an electrical shock? This only goes to show that electrical energy is in the hands; the hands have the power to heal or to curse.

The Hebrew language, in which every letter has a characteristic meaning, the letter (character) Yod, means hand,

> *"Thy hand (Yod) hath made me and*
> *fashioned me: give me understanding that I*
> *may learn thy commandments." Ps. 119.73*

Even a person's feet can bring forth blessings or curses, can bring positive or negative conditions into one's life, depending on where one allows his or her feet to take them. The feet are the final station in the body of the inflow of the electro- magnetic pole of the law of polarity. The feet tell if the body is well or sick; if the feet hurt, the whole body hurts.

> *"Thy word is a lamp unto my feet, and a*
> *light unto my path." Psalms 119.105*

> *"Blessed is the man (or woman) that*
> *walketh not in the counsel of the*
> *unrighteous, nor standeth in the way of*
> *sinners, nor sitteth in the seat of the*
> *scornful. But his delight is in the law of*
> *Yahweh; and in His law (instructions) doth*
> *he meditate day and night. And he shall be*
> *like a tree planted by the rivers of the water,*
> *that bringeth forth his fruit in his season; his*
> *leaf also shall not whither; and whatsoever*
> *he doeth shall prosper." Psalms 1.1-3*

THE POWER THAT FLOWS FROM THE MOST HIGH CREATOR (YAHWEH EL-ELYON)

Yahweh is the creative spiritual power, all great, all knowing, and everywhere present, which lives, moves and breathes in the smallest atoms, protons, neutrons, electrons, and all other energy bases that have been kept hidden in relation to the universe. Yahweh is El Gedolah, the Great Power, and unlimited creativity, the Eheiyeh or All Existing Power Which Wills Everything into Existence and vibrates at this very moment through your human body. (`For in Him do we live and move and have our being.`) You will feel and use this spiritual energy through the power of the name Yahweh, which has deliberately been blotted out of your awareness. All space around us everywhere is charged with this mighty power of Yahweh

El-Elyon, the Most High Power. We, however, can never know or use this invisible current or power until we personally contact this energy and consciously claim our share according to the measure of our needs. In your own vivid awareness and acceptance of this power is the secret to your success in the world.

> *"Yahweh is not the Elohim of the dead, but of the living."* Matt. 22.32.

> *"Yahweh is spirit."* John 4.24.

> *"He that loveth not, knoweth not Yahweh, for Yahweh is love."* I John 4.8.

> *"Yahweh is Light and in Him is no darkness at all."* I John 1.5.

This light that is Yahweh enters the human heart like a sunray. By means of the Neshamah, the soul, this light mixes and amalgamates with the fluids of your body, the blood, the nerve currents, and permeates every organ of your body in the form of what we call Life. Yahweh is light, but the light that is Yahweh is beyond our human mental comprehension and so cannot be called a conceivable light. But as this light enters the mind it becomes intellectual light to you and so you can then mentally comprehend it. Of course this light is without form or body and when it enters into the soul it takes form but is invisible to the physical eye. Yet as it penetrates your physical organism it becomes visible also to the outer perception. The greatest manifestation of this light in the physical world came in the form of Yahoshua the Messiah.

"In the beginning was the Word, and the Word was with Yahweh, and the Word was Yahweh. The same was in the beginning with Yahweh. All things were made by Him; and without Him was not anything that was made. In him was life; and the life was the

light of men. And the light shineth in darkness; and the darkness comprehended it not. There was a man sent from Yahweh, whose name was John. These same came for a witness, to bear witness of the Light, that all men through Him might believe. He was not that Light, but was sent to bear witness of that Light. The true Light was that which lighteth every man that cometh into the world. He was in the world, and the world was made by Him, and the world knew Him not. He came unto His own tribe, and His own people received Him not. But as many as received Him, to them gave He power to become the children of Yahweh; that is to them that believe on the Name of Him, who was born, not of blood, nor of the will of man, but of Yahweh. And the word was made flesh and dwelt among us, (and we beheld His glory, the glory of the only begotten of the Father), full of grace and truth." St. John 1.1-14

"And we know that we are of Yahweh." I
John 5.19

"Ye are the temple of the living Yahweh."
II Corinthians 6.16.

Change your thinking about Yahweh and you will
change your world. Know that the creative law of Yahweh
is the law of fulfillment. When we turn to the Bible, we
find that the prophets of old certainly proclaimed Yahweh
as the Yahweh of riches - spiritual as well as earthly.

> *"Every man also to whom Elohim hath*
> *given riches and easy wealth, and hath given*
> *him power to eat thereof and to take his*
> *portion, and to rejoice in his labor; this is*
> *the gift of Yahweh." Ecc. 5.19.*
>
> *"Both riches and honor come of Thee and*
> *Thou reignest over all; and in Thine hand it*
> *is to make great and to give strength unto*
> *all." I Chron 29.12.*
>
> *"And Elohim, The Almighty Creator, said*
> *`Let us make man in our image." Gen 1.26.*

Yahweh Elohim is a spirit and you were made in His
image. You are Life of His Life, Mind of His Mind, Spirit
of His Spirit, Substance of His Substance. You must realize
that, *`Before Abraham was, I was,'* (we use the word 'was'
in place of the 'am' because it is a more correct translation
of the original Hebraic text), meaning that you did not
begin with birth and you will not end with death. In the
beginning was the Word, which involved the whole scheme
of creation; that scheme included you. The real you was
present and was one with Yahweh Elohim, the Almighty
Creator, when the world was thought into being. *`Thou*

sawest my substance before I was formed in my mother's womb,' is an ancient way of telling us that even the material body was created from the realms of spiritual substance. Though it is true that your body and mind find limitations, there are times of inspiration when your spirit can rise above all obstacles and can achieve awesome results in the face of all your seeming imitations. Faithful study and following every direction given throughout these pages will help you master, direct, and command this inspiration at will, even as Yahoshua the Messiah did, who was a high priest after the Order of Melchizedek.

In the creative beginning of earthly time, from the Atsilutic World, the World of Existence, Yahweh chose to attribute Himself into countless millions of living units, and as a result, each human being exists as a separate individual. Each individual is endowed with not only a human or earthly rate of vibration, but also with individual endowment from the spiritual realms. You can develop and use Yahweh's spiritual essence just as easily and just as certainly as you can develop and use your individual mental faculties. Yahweh working through universal energy and the universal substance of all animate and inanimate creation vibrates in harmony with the energy and substance in you. But as long as you live on the purely physical and mental planes or levels of consciousness, just so long will this limitless, powerful energy and substance remain dormant, inactive, and unused in you because you have excluded the greatest power in the world from your awareness. Because He is truly Yahweh Gedolah, El-Shaddai, the Powerful and All Sufficient One, *"He giveth power to the faint; and to them that have no might, He increaseth strength."* Is. 40.29

When you realize and show faith in its reality, you can

draw from Yahweh El-Elyon, the Most High Power, as much as you can faithfully accept. It is a never failing force which will manifest through you in an ever increasing and greater fullness as you keep your thought vibration attuned to the right current. Call those wandering thoughts to a focal point and rely entirely upon Yahweh El-Elyon, the Most High Power, which flows into you from the unseen Azilutic World, the World of Existence. Just in proportion as you expand your conception of Yahweh, in that same proportion your relation to Him expands and your harmony with higher vibrations is perfected day by day.

Picture an electric light bulb. It shines with a white light, but suppose the globe is painted an opaque black? If it is night and no other light shines in the room, darkness results, but the light does not cease. Within the light bulb the light shines just as it did before, but the light can no longer express itself as light to your eyes. Many would conclude that no light is present, yet in reality the light is still there. Now scratch a small circle of the black paint from the light bulb and a little light begins to shine through. As you keep on scratching paint from the bulb, the volume of light grows. The light represents your mental concept of Yahweh which is expressed exactly in accordance with the conception your own thinking applies to Him.

> *"Neither do men light a candle, and put it under a bushel, but on a candlestick, and it giveth light unto all that are in the house."* Matt. 5.15.

Picture yourself as a magnet drawing all that you need from the outer worlds: the Azilutic World of Existence, the realms of pure will, where all that is, that was, and that is to be exists, from the Briah World of Creation and Manifestation, where things take on animated form but cannot be physically seen, flowing into the Yitzirah World of Formation, where spirit takes on tangible form and can be physically seen depending upon a person's level of vibration, sifting throughout the Asiyah World of Manifestation, where liquids, gases, and solids are formed. Your power to draw from these worlds will increase day by day as the force of demand increases.

In the many teachings of The Order of Melchizedek, as revealed in the holy scriptures, great space is given to certain teachings and parables. The real lesson is deeply hidden in allegory and symbolism. Everywhere hidden within the allegory and the symbolism of the ancient teaching is the simple truth that the eternal law of Yahweh El-Elyon, the Most High Power, does not act throughout this universe to provide for your needs in some perfect and mystical land beyond the clouds after you are dead. This great power offers you all that you need here and now if you will only learn to obey the everlasting law of the universe and accept it into your life with confidence and faith.

The word mystery is used in the New Covenant many times and in every case this word has the same meaning - a secret which was given only to those students who had been prepared by proper instruction to receive and to understand it. To the students of old the word mystery meant a hidden truth to be had for the searching. These students were prepared by long ceremonials of initiation to receive and grasp this information. Much of these mysteries are being revealed today. Many of Yahoshua's words are proof that this was His method of instructing His disciples, *"Unto you is given to know the mysteries of the Kingdom of Yahweh, but not unto all." Matt. 13.11.*

The purpose for sharing this information is to bring to you the spiritual as well as the scientific truth that the same creative power which created this universe is everywhere around you and vibrates within you; it is everywhere invisible and everywhere the most dynamic form of power in existence. When you consciously and sincerely open your spirit and mind to receive this invisible creative power then every desire that you can picture with faith and confidence will materialize into your life in ever increasing amounts. You can form, you can create, you can attract to yourself what you will and what you most desire from the Atsilutic World of Existence. Expand your thinking and build your faith in Yahweh. Can you open your mind to believe in things which the world calls impossible? Can you soar beyond the limitations of the mental and physical planes to believe in miracles?

"Now a certain man was sick, named Lacers, of Bethany, the town of Miriam and her sister Martha. (It was that Miriam which anointed Yahoshua with ointment, and wiped His feet with her hair, whose brother was sick.) Therefore his sisters sent unto Him, saying, Rabbi, behold, he whom thou loves is sick. When Yahoshua heard that, He said, this sickness is not unto death, but for the glory of Yahweh, that the Son of Yahweh might be glorified thereby. Now Yahoshua loved Martha, and her sister, and Lazarus. When he had heard therefore, that he was sick, He abode two days still in the same place where He was.

Then after that, saith he to His disciples, Let us go into Judea again. His disciples said unto Him, Rabbi, the Jews of late sought to stone thee; and goest Thou tither again?

Yahoshua answered, `are there not twelve hours unto the day? If any man walk in the day, he stumbleth not, because he seeth the light of this world. But if a man walk in the night, he stumbleth, because there is no light in it. These things said He: and after that He saith unto them, Our friend Lazarus sleepeth; but I go, that I may awake him out of sleep. Then said His disciples, Rabbi, if he sleep, he shall do well. Howbeit Yahoshua spake of his death: but they thought that he had spoken of taking rest in sleep. Then said Yahoshua unto them plainly, Lazarus is dead. And I am glad for your sakes that I was not there, to the intent ye may believe; nevertheless let us go unto him. Then said Thomas, which is called Didymus, unto his fellow disciples, Let us also go, that we may die with him. Then when Yahoshua came, He found that he had lain in the grave four days already. Now Bethany was nigh unto Jerusalem about two miles: And many of the Jews came to Martha and Miriam, to comfort them concerning their brother. Then Martha, as soon as she heard that Yahoshua was coming, went and met Him: but Miriam was still in the house. Then said Martha unto Yahoshua, Rabbi, if Thou hadst been here, my Brother had not died. But I know, that even now, whatsoever though wilt ask of Yahweh, He will give it to thee. Yahoshua said to her, thy brother shall rise again. Martha *said unto him, I know that he shall rise again, in the resurrection at the last day. Yahoshua said unto her, I am the resurrection and the life: he that believeth in Me, though he were dead, yet shall he live: And whosoever liveth and believeth in Me shall not die for ever; believest thou this? She said unto him, `Yea, I believe that Thou art the Messiah, the Son of Yahweh, which should come into the world.' And when she so said, she went her way and called Miriam, her sister, secretly saying, the Rabbi is come, and calleth thee. As soon as she heard that, she arose quickly, and came unto Him. Now Yahoshua was not yet come into the town, but was in that place where Martha met him. The Jews which were with her in the house comforted her when they saw Miriam that she arose up hastily and went out, followed her saying, `she goeth unto the grave to weep there.' Then when Miriam was come where Yahoshua was, and saw him, she fell down at his feet, saying unto Him, Rabboni, if thou hadst been here, my brother had not died. When Yahoshua therefore saw her weeping, and the Jews also weeping which came with her; He groaned in the spirit and was troubled. And said, Where have ye laid him? They said unto Him, Rabbi, come and see. Yahoshua wept. Then said the Jews, Behold how He loved him! And some of them said, could not this man which opened the eyes of the blind, have caused that even this man should not have died? Yahoshua therefore again groaning in himself cometh to the grave. It was a cave, and* *a stone lay upon it. Yahoshua said take ye away the stone. Martha, the sister of him that was dead, saith unto Him, Rabbi, why are they lifting away the stone? By this time he stinketh; for he hath been dead four days. Yahoshua saith unto her, `said I not unto thee, that if thou wouldest believe, thou shouldest see the glory of Yahweh? Then they took away the stone from the place where the dead was laid. And Yahoshua lifted up His eyes and said, Father, I thank thee that Thou has heard Me. And I knew that Thou hearest me always: but because of the people which stand by I said it, that they may believe that thou hast sent me. And when He thus had spoken, He cried with a loud voice, Lazarus, come forth. And he that was dead came forth, bound hand and foot with grave clothes and his face was bound about with a napkin. Yahoshua said unto them, loose him and let him go. Then many of the Jews which came to Miriam, and had seen the things Yahoshua did, believed on Him." St. John 11.1-45.*

"Verily, verily, I say unto you, he that believeth on me, the works that I do shall he do also; and greater works than these shall he do; because I go unto My Father." St. John 14.12.

Spirit works its miracle in your life by the power of faith. Faith is an unshakable confidence, an unwavering expectation, based upon your knowledge that you are in essence the materialized form of Yahweh El-Elyon, and the power that flows from you can be used to achieve great and wonderful things.

All around us in this world are sounds which the human ear can never hear and there are radiations in the air everywhere which we cannot see or feel, but when we transform these radiations into sound waves, as with the radio, the we can hear what we cannot see or feel. These radiations (vibrations) while invisible and inaudible, constantly travel through any material. Certain words are a radiation of extraordinary power. Moses, the instruction giver of the Hebrew Scripture, an initiate of the secret wisdom of the Egyptians and educated in their temples, so long ago gave us a plain and simple statement about Yahweh in words that give a deep meaning to the hidden power of the name of Elohim. *"Thus shalt thou say unto the children of Israel, EHEIYEH ASHER EHEIYEH, (I am the Self Existent One, who Wills what He wills to Be), Yahweh is My Name forever."* Ex. 3.14-15.

Again it is stated in Deuteronomy 6.14, *"Hear, Oh Israel, Yahweh is Our Strength, Yahweh is Unity (Accad)."* Hebraic translation renders the word, normally written as 'one' as unity. Take, for example a cluster of grapes, you will find many units of them on one cluster, all with the same essence. They are a unity and so likewise is Yahweh and all His attributes. So, I WILL BE, is unity and there is no second. I WILL BE WHAT I WILL TO BE, YAHWEH, is the unity that does all things. The highest expression toward you of Yahweh El-Elyon, the Most High Power, is Love, and this Love grants your greatest desires and blesses you with material wealth and spiritual fulfillment.

The Power of Unity:

"I will to be one with Yahweh El-Elyon, the Most High Power."

"I will to be one with Yahweh Ropheka, the Healer."

"I will to be one with Yahweh El-Shaddai, the All Sufficient Provider, Nourisher, Sustainer."

SPIRITUAL MAGNETISM:

Spiritual Magnetism is commonly referred to as Character. It is the impression you make upon other people, and it determines what other people think of you. Their opinion of you is formed by the impression your character makes upon them. Here is an example to illustrate the affect of character. One day a woman entered the dining room of a large hotel. Two women who were at their table talking noticed the woman who had come in and commented on her attractiveness. Although she was surrounded by friends, she stood out among them. She filled the room with her presence. The waiters were unusually attentive to her. She was not what many might call beautiful and her clothes were neither striking nor costly, but the effect of her character set her apart from the other women in the room. She was radiant.

The world avoids negative beings and instinctively recoils from them, and the great mass of people are doomed to live unnoticed and frustrated lives because of negative and colorless beings. The two great classes of beings into which all men and women are divided are those who are colorful, interesting and attractive and those who are drab, dull, and easily forgotten. It is important to keep in mind that an attractive character is not a peculiar gift given at birth and it is not limited to the few. Acquiring a magnetic and active character requires understanding and work. A charming, winning, and magnetic character must be developed.

Character and success are partners. Think back and you may recall that whatever success you have had in life was because you were either able to impress men or women of influence with your superior talent, or because you attracted the friendship or support of those who could properly promote you, or who had the power to open doors of opportunity for you. To win success it was necessary for you to make favorable impressions upon other people.

Consider the saying, *"Clothes do not make the man."* This may be true in the real meaning of the term, but we must consider that proper grooming can attract to a person favorable attention and consideration which he would otherwise never receive. The style and quality of your clothes is a very important part of your character, and it is a fact that people form impressions of you based upon your outward appearance. While it is true that some people have achieved great success in life who were extremely careless about their dress, these few attained such power of character that they succeeded in spite of and not because of their clothes. The effect of your dress is double. First, there is the very noticeable effect upon yourself, and second, the impression that your clothes make upon others. Suitable clothing can protect you from fear; you can defeat fear by the attractive power of a well dressed character.

Many books have been written about that seemingly mysterious something called personal magnetism, but when we come to analyze it we find that personal magnetism is a very simple quality. This something about which there has been so much mystery is nothing more than being genuinely interested in people and letting that sincere human interest shine forth in your words and your deeds. Give out real friendship, radiate a warm interest in everyone around you and everywhere along life's pathway you will find helping friendly hearts assisting you to gain success. Never forget that the most interesting subject to man is himself and all people love admiration. When you take an interest in other human beings, they automatically reciprocate by taking a sincere interest in you. We are attracted to those who are attracted to us. To develop personal magnetism it is highly essential that you make a habit of studying others closely enough so as to find something in them that is admirable. Not the cheap flattery that is easily detected by those who are perceptive, but the sincere admiration stemming from keen observation of that which is good.

The foundation upon which a pleasing, magnetic character is based is a sound, positive character. We telegraph who we are through the nature of our character. You may embellish your character with fine clothes, with a beautiful smile, and with a pleasing manner, but if your character is permeated with hatred, greed, envy, malice, jealousy and selfishness, you will never attract, but instead repel; others will discern intuitively who you really are and will feel that beyond the pleasing exterior there is something about you that is not quite right or wholesome.

A sound, wholesome character can be developed by modeling the qualities of those people with the particular characteristics you desire. A very effective way to build the desired qualities in your character is to visualize yourself possessing them. During your periods of meditation, visualize yourself in situations where these qualities may be acted out. Suggest to yourself in clear, precise language, that you are now developing these qualities in yourself. There are several creative and imaginative ways in which you can make this happen. One way is to place the person with the qualities you wish to possess directly in front of you. Affirm that you wish to build within your own character the qualities they possess. Seal the impression by declaring that you now possess the qualities you seek. Whenever an occasion arises in your life in which you are given the opportunity to practice the new quality, act upon it without hesitation. The first step in the information on mastering fear is - before all else, act. Another technique you may wish to use is to visualize the people with the qualities you wish to possess seated with you at a table. Compliment each one for being an example, a positive role model and state to each one the qualities they possess, which you wish to build within your own character. You may have each one of them bless you in the name of Yahweh El-Shaddai, the All Sufficient Provider, and seal the impression by saying, *"It is done in the name and through the power that is in the name of Yahoshua the*

Messiah. " You may use these examples or choose your own. Whatever you decide to do, be sure that you believe that it can and will be done.

In all that you do related to developing an attractive character, control of your thinking is most important; control your thinking so that your thoughts are constantly focused on the person you desire to be. As many times a day as possible direct your thoughts to the images of the models of solid, healthy character that you have chosen. Sit with them, see them, study them, and know with perfect faith that what you seek to develop within yourself will surely manifest.

If you will earnestly apply the method given here in a disciplined way, with perseverance and faith, you will notice a transformation in your character that may surprise you. This transformation is entirely within your control.

Mirror Exercise: In the ancient teachings of the Zohar, the Book of Splendor, passed down from Moses and the ancient sages, it is explained that our face reveals our character and it tells the world everything about who we are. Practice the mirror exercise and with a determined purpose, judge fairly and impartially the impression you think you make upon others at the present time. Mirrors can be referred to as a looking glass for the mind, one that shows not only the external form, but also the quality of the character. You are standing before this looking glass to see the true visage and complexion of your soul. Without an introspective approach (with or without the mirror) you cannot know the truth of who you really are. Your mirror will inform you from day to day of your progress in attaining magnetic power and it will reflect plainly each and every improvement you make in your inner development and outward appearance.

In your search for admirable qualities in others, be sure that when you have found some good quality, that you give sincere praise of it. What this does is develop in you the habit of respecting and giving honor to others, and they in turn intuit a wholesomeness in your character and you in turn will be praised, honored and respected.

MASTERING FEAR

*"Be not afraid of sudden fear; neither of the
desolation of the wicked, when it cometh,
For Yahweh shall be thy confidence, and
shall keep thy foot from being taken." Pr.
3.25*

Let us call attention to the deep wisdom of these words
of King Solomon:

*"Keep thy heart with all diligence; for out of
it are the issues (results) of life." Prov.
4.23.*

Remember that the Messiah almost always spoke in parables and symbols and that beneath the surface His words contained hidden meaning. We have this specific warning from His lips *"And a man's foes shall be they of his own (mental) household."* *Matthew 10.36.* We can discern that Solomon's use of the word `heart' symbolically means mind and likewise Yahoshua's use of the word `household' symbolizes thought. Of the enemies within your own household - foes of your progress and of your spiritual development - fear leads all the rest. If you open your mind to fear and allow it to remain there, your most deadly enemy will weave the pattern of failure into the very fiber of your mind and just as surely will it materialize by degrees in your outer physical world. Many ghosts, all imaginary, have come to haunt men and women throughout the ages, but out of them all, fear has always held a most terrible power because it paralyzes action. Unless it is mastered, it actually freezes the blood of accomplishment in the veins of those who fear. The pity of it all is that ninety percent of our fears are groundless, unreal and imaginary. Fear is behind every failure. Every human failure is a tribute to fear, whether we know it or not and has even caused the physical death of millions of its victims. This fear degrades life and enslaves manhood and womanhood. Have you been afraid to stand alone and have you trembled for fear that others might not approve of your stand? Such a mental fear forces conformity and robs your life of spontaneity and freedom of expression. Fearlessness, on the other hand, is the divine quality which the great soul must possess.

Have you ever heard the ancient story of the plague? The Plague was returning from a city where he had used an epidemic to kill a hundred thousand people and on the way he met his colleague Famine. Famine, desirous to please Plague, said admiringly, `I must commend you, brother, on the fine work you have done - killing a hundred thousand people is quite an accomplishment!' `I did not kill a hundred thousand people, growled Plague,' impatient with the ignorance of Famine, `I only killed ten thousand, the others died of Fear, go commend him about the rest!'

Your fears are the products of your emotional nature, so you must make a concerted effort to control your emotions. When you learn to do this you can master every fear. Deep within every one of us lurks the heritage of fear which we inherited from our ancestors. When you master fear you have done a great thing - you have triumphed over an inbred instinct of mankind. If you were to analyze the weaknesses, errors, habits, beliefs, and powerful desires which the average man is beset with, you will discover that fear plays a part at every level. Fear has impelled man to develop some of his most precious gifts, has given impetus to many great reforms, and has saved man from activities which are self destructive, but there comes a stage in man's development when fear must be superseded by Love and Wisdom.

It is important for you to realize how much time and energy which could be put to more constructive use and employed in strengthening your body and calming your mind, are wasted through the anticipation of situations, misfortunes, and failures, many of which never materialize.

Yahoshua the Messiah mastered fear to such an extent that He was able to have power over the force of nature:

"And, behold, there arose a great tempest in the sea, inasmuch that the ship was covered with the waves: but He was asleep. And His disciples came to Him, and awoke Him, saying, Rabbi, save us: we perish. And He saith unto them, Why are ye fearful, O ye of little faith? Then He arose, and rebuked the winds and the sea; and there was a great calm. And the men marvelled, saying, What manner of Man is This that even the winds and the sea obey Him!" (Matt. 8.23-27).

Will you perish in the face of the tempest or will you have the faith and therefore the power to rebuke it?

Many of the things people dread and which, in consequence weaken their resolve and fortitude, become powerful emotional blocks which prevent positive action and influence their thinking in advance to opportunities and situations when they arise. If such thought forms are constantly created and brooded upon they can become so charged with magnetic force that they tend to draw to their creator the very experience he dreads. So remember, when you make persistent pictures of your inability to deal with any given situation or problem that you are actually injecting into it negative energy which will tend to create the climate in which your fears are most likely to materialize. Until you reach the stage where you know for sure that Yahweh Elohim, the Almighty Creator is your ever present help, try to practice habitually the transformation of destructive into constructive thinking until it becomes a habit. An extremely important method of dealing with negative thoughts is by a deliberate attempt to focus attention elsewhere. Attention is one of the most powerful ways of concentrating energy upon some specific focus. Also, concentration upon the present, rather than spending time worrying about a hypothetical future, helps to modify your course towards the more positive ends you wish to see manifest in your life.

If we could succeed in banishing exaggerated insecurity and fear from the earth, we would double the health and happiness of the human race. Strong impressions of terror or bouts of fear and anxiety, whether they come from conversation, a vivid imagination, the movies or the headlines, leave a residue in the soul and when this feeling invades an idle mind it tends to fill it with anxiety. These are images which actually cause organic changes such as physical inhibitions, trembling, contraction of the blood vessels, palpitations and so on. The more vague and confused the fear, the more it afflicts us. We must drag it out from its hidden cave, look at it face to face and then we can destroy it. The idea or apprehension of danger whether real or imaginary is the cause of fear, and its consequent inhibitions keep increasing in proportion to the magnitude of the danger and the difficulty of avoiding it. If we walk out in front of an audience with all eyes on us, very few of us will walk naturally. We are literally shaken up, and if the serious danger or misfortune seems to be inevitable, then anxiety tends to destroy all control of movements, ideas, and emotions. Even the memory can be inhibited as when the timid student takes an examination. Paralysis of all our powers may follow if the fear is extremely great. An example of this is the confusion and witless panic that often comes with an earthquake or a fire in a theater.

Fear is the emotion most difficult to control because often we do not know what we fear and why we are afraid. In such cases, a deep exploration, a diligent investigation of the fear is necessary. We may take the following steps to conquer fear:

Before all else, act. Fear already tends to inhibit our activities. So we must not assist it by remaining inactive but conquer it by acting.

Make them concrete. We must illuminate the fear. Drag it right out into the open and examine it. Calmly, reasonably, and impartially analyze this emotion which has cost you so much. Mentally pick this fear to pieces and scrutinize each part carefully. In dealing with this fear, don't pay any attention to its pretenses or it's whimpers. Use the same emotional power which you have been wasting on fear to build faith into your life. Fear runs away in terror in the face of faith. Answer these questions in writing and in detail: Just what am I afraid of? And why? When fear of anxiety is made concrete and viewed objectively, then it can be destroyed.

Reason about them. What probabilities are there that this thing will really happen? And if it does happen, will it really be as disastrous as I fear?

Face up to them. Supposing that this happens, then what? So what? Are there not others who have gone through similar crises? Haven't they gone on living and become successful and happy? When we imagine the worst possible natural evil that could happen to us and sincerely accept it and find a human or spiritual solution for it, we will be victorious over exaggerated fear.

Deliberately affirm contrary judgments, e.g., 'There is no special danger in this' or 'the probability that this will happen is very small.' Even if it does happen the disadvantage would be insignificant or at least there would come with it several advantages which would far counterbalance it.

Deliberately foster contrary feelings of courage or security. This is done by exhibiting intense acts of courage, by vivid remembrances of peaceful moments or places, by actually saying something in a tone of courage or security in the voice.

Associate this reliving of past peaceful moments with the circumstance which had been producing anxiety in you. Imagine that you are in control of the situation and that you are speaking in a masterful tone of voice.

Work on muscular constriction. A latent state of insecurity or anxiety due to strong and prolonged tension in the muscles prevents the quiet easy expansion of the chest which is normal when we are secure and feeling good. This tension causes us to assume a posture characteristic of timidity or depression. The state that we assume is very much a result of the way we picture and say things to ourselves as well as how we use our physical bodies. The mind and body are totally linked, so that the way you use your physiology - the way you breath, your posture, your facial expression - actually determine the state you are in. Therefore, making an effort to loosen the muscles and free constricted energy points in the body through exercise of various sorts, maintaining an upright posture, reflecting confidence, assuming the opposite facial expression, keeping the voice steady and firm, maintaining breathing that is deep and slow, all these aid in mastering fear.

What begins as timidity or cowardice can degenerate into feelings of inferiority or an inferiority complex. This depressive feeling of inferiority drags millions of men and women down and robs them of courage, faith, and happiness. The people around them do not believe in them because they will not believe in themselves. Often their real abilities never have a chance to demonstrate in achievement because they doubt their own power so much that they are afraid to even attempt the very activities which would raise them to the heights of success. They are paralyzed by this feeling of lack in themselves. Because he hates himself, the man who lives with inferiority always lives in the wretchedness of self-abnegation. Sometimes a little self-hatred (i.e. hating the negative attributes of one's character) can lead to spiritual growth, but true inferiority complexes are not temporary and the man suffering from such a mental state is always convinced that he is inferior in all ways to all people. Inferiority in a person may be due to a very large number of reasons. It may be due to a person being given little or no expression of security of their character during infancy or adolescence. Perhaps his education was overly protective and warded off from him every exposure to difficulty or danger. He may have grown up in a hostile and derogatory environment, i.e. racism, sexism, etc. (Compounded by media images, television, movies, books, magazines....). Or other people may have always made decisions for him, and he never became accustomed to assuming responsibility himself. Or it may have been due to a frequent experience of fear which was not countered immediately by positive thoughts and so the fear remained at a subconscious level. It may come from a false concept of inferiority because of some past failure. It may be grounded upon some real defect or a real incapacity in some particular field, which his imagination extends to other areas while hiding away his real talents and good qualities. It may be due to excessive ambition or to the kind of depression that results from seeking unrealistic goals. He may be a man seeking human success without giving importance to success in the eyes of his Creator. In other words, whoever seeks delight in fulfilling the will of

Yahweh Elohim, the Almighty Creator, can find satisfaction in life even though human success may seem to fail at that moment. Sometimes feelings of inferiority may come from irrational panic about, 'what will they say,' or fear of ridicule. A sense of inferiority is sometimes the result of comparing oneself with others. This is especially liable to happen if a person is involved with others who are better prepared or highly talented. In such a situation, it is important to think of the fact that everyone is given gifts from Yahweh Elohim, the Almighty Creator. You must develop to the fullest, the gifts given to you at birth.

If you find this fear in yourself, begin to diligently use the steps outlined to overcome it. There is no reason for fear. Take courage at every victory often repeating, '*I am going to win. Each time I have more courage.*' Never use negative formulas or conjure up the memory of phobias or symptoms which disturbed you. If you say, for instance, '*I am not going to tremble,*' you will produce the very effect you wish to avoid.

Stir up your faith in Yahweh Elohim, the Almighty Creator, who appreciates us, loves us, and is always there to help us. Draw your conclusion from this: Humble yes, timid no, '*for I can do all things in Him who strengthens me.*' Yahweh Elohim, the Almighty Creator, commands us not to fear, '*not to even those who can kill the body.*' Confident and persevering prayer receives whatever it asks for, so pray and have faith that your prayer is answered. Keep in mind that "*the effectual fervent prayer of a righteous man availeth much.*" *James 5.16.* However, bear deeply in mind, '*even so faith, if it hath not works, is dead.*' *James 2.17.*

When you reach a stage of genuinely accepting the existence of a stronger than human center of energy -

Yahweh Elohim, the Almighty Creator - within yourself, which can and should be called upon for help and inspiration, then the whole situation is bound to alter, for you know for sure that you no longer walk or fight alone.

The Power of Thought:

> *"Whatever does not conquer me makes me stronger."*

Just as knowing how to fall correctly is necessary for certain sports, also for victory in life. We must know how to win even when we are beaten. We must learn how to fall without discouragement, to lose without irritation, to fail without despair, to suffer without sadness:

> *"I can do all things in Him who strengthens me."*

> *"If Yahweh be with us, who shall stand against us? If the Almighty is with me, whom shall I fear?"*

> *"If I learn how to profit from the lessons, even defeat will be transformed into strength."*

> *"No failure should cause me to lose a joyful and optimistic hope for the eventual success of my undertakings."*

> *"The power of the Almighty Creator, Yahweh Elohim, is my shield from all harm."*

"Yahweh is my light and my salvation, whom shall I fear? Yahweh is the strength of my life, of whom shall I be afraid?" "Hast thou not known, hast thou not heard, that the Everlasting Elohim, Yahweh, the Creator of the ends of the earth fainteth not, neither is weary? There is no searching of His understanding. He giveth power to the faint; and to them that have no might. He increaseth strength. Though youth shall faint and be weary, and the young men shall utterly fail: But they that wait upon Yahweh shall renew their strength; they shall mount up with wings as eagles; they shall run, and not be weary; and they shall walk, and not faint."
Is 40.28-31

TO THE ONE-HUNDRED &
FORTY-FOUR THOUSAND

*"And after these things, I saw four angels
(Uriel, Michael, Gabriel, Raphael) standing
on the four corners of the earth restraining
the four winds (spirits) of the earth that the
winds should not blow on the earth, nor on
the sea, nor on any tree. And I saw another
angel ascending from the east, having the
seal of the living Elohim: and He called
with a loud voice to the four angels, to
whom it was given to hurt the earth and the
sea, saying `Hurt not the earth, neither the
sea, neither the trees, till we have sealed the
servants of our Elohim in their foreheads.
And I heard the number of them which were*

sealed: and there were sealed a hundred and forty-four thousand of all the tribes of the children of Israel." Rev. 7. 1-4

"And I looked and lo, a lamb stood on Mount Zion, and with him a hundred and forty and four-thousand having His Name and His Father's Name written in their forehead." Rev. 14.1

- **100 = Kof,** which means back of the head; the medulla oblongata (in the back of the head) is the source of material or physical awareness.

- **40 = Mem** - which means water or spirit.

- **4 = Daleth** - indicating the crossing of a threshold.

- **1,000 = Alef** - association or advancement.

The mystery of the 144,000 in the scriptural phrase, should read as follows: *'Those who succeed in advancing their consciousness from the state of material awareness (back of the head) to the state of spiritual awareness (forehead, the location of the third eye, called Ayana Chakra), they are the ones who shall redeem themselves, or gain the freedom of their divine higher nature.'*

I, Melchizedek the Prophet, await you in the land of Israel, to teach you and guide you on how to become sealed by the Holy Spirit with the Holy Name of the Father and the Son - in spirit and in truth - before the close of this age.

Only those that are chosen will be inspired to come to the Holy Land and seek out the presence of Melchizedek Ha Nabi, the Prophet King of Righteousness. The keys of

Divine Knowledge will be transmitted to the human family by the Order of Melchizedek, to become a unity of light.

The Jerusalem Command of the Order of Melchizedek will establish academies of Light so as to prepare the vibratory field of the spiritual body to acclimate the physical body and mind for rapid changes, defying negative thought patterns. We will be given a thorough comprehensive understanding of how we can use our five bodies of light - 1) 'Overself' (the higher-self), 2) Electro-magnetic, 3) Gematron, 4) Light Body, the 5) 'Bio-Chemical,' and Spiritual gifts to prepare for the New World:

"Now there are diversities of gifts, but the same spirit. And there are diversities of administrations, but the same Elohim. There are diversities of operations, but it is the same Elohim that worketh all in all. But the manifestation of the spirit is given to every man to profit withall. For to the one it is given by the spirit the word of wisdom; to another the word of knowledge by the same spirit; to another faith by the same spirit; to another the gift of healing by the same spirit; to another the workings of miracles and to another prophecy; to another discerning of spirits; to another various kinds of tongues; to another the interpretation of tongues: But all of these worketh that one in the self same spirit, dividing to every man severly as he will. . . And Yahweh had sent some into the assemblies, first apostles, secondly prophets, thirdly teachers, then workers of miracles, then healers, helpers, administrators, speakers in various kinds of tongues." I Cor. 12.4-11, 28.

"And though I have the gift of prophecy and understand all mysteries, and all knowledge; and though I have all faith, so that I could remove mountains, and have not love, I am nothing." I Cor. 13.2.

"Follow after love, and desire spiritual gifts, but rather that you may prophecize." I Cor. 14.1

The Order of Melchizedek will give light to all areas of universal spiritual truth so that the New Covenant of Yahweh will manifest, activating a spiritual synthesis. Those who are chosen to come to Jerusalem to be taught by Melchizedek will become the active recipients who promulgate the Law of the Living Light, as it is written: *'The law shall go forth out of Zion, and the Word of Yahweh from Jerusalem." Micah 4.1-2.* This Light will come forth from Spiritual Israel, the coordination of all races of man, so that all mankind can be brought to salvation from the kingdoms of flesh into the kingdoms of light.

Come let us remove ourselves from the pharaohs of the world, the pharaohs who keep the world in slavery and economic bondage, without the capstone of light. Come let us cleanse the system of life and exalt Yahweh who divides the heavens and the earth through His people. . . In the Holy Name of Yahweh El-Elyon, I await you. . .I await you. . . I await you. . . I await you. Selah.

THE BENEFITS OF FASTING

Renew yourself and Fast. Remember that from the time when He created the heavens, YAHWEH Elohim created the Fast for a benefit to men on account of the passions and desires which fight against you so that the evil will not inflame you. "But it is a pure fast which Yahweh have created," the one who Fasts continually will not sin although jealously and strife one within him. Let the pure one Fast, but whenever the one who Fasts is not pure he has angered YAHWEH and also the angels. And he has grieved his soul, gathering up wrath for himself for the day of wrath." *Apocalypse of Elijah I 15-20, OT Pseudopigrapha*

"But a pure Fast is what YAHWEH created, with a pure heart and pure hands. It releases sin. It heals diseases. It is effective up to the throne of YAHWEH for an ointment and for a release from sin by means of a pure prayer." Isa. 58:3-6

"Hear, O' wise men who has been chosen, concerning the deceivers who will multiply in the last times so that they will set down for themselves doctrines which do not belong to YAHWEH, setting aside the LAW OF YAHWEH. Those who have made their belly their EL, saying 'The Fast does not exist, nor did Yahweh create it,' making themselves strangers to the covenant of YAHWEH and robbing themselves of the glorious promises. Now these are not ever correctly established in and with firm faith. Therefore, don't let those people lead you astray." Phil 3:19.

For I tell you truly, that Satan and his plagues may only be cast out by Fasting and by prayer. Matt. 17:19-21.

"Go by yourself and Fast alone, and show your Fasting to no man." Matt. 6:18. *YAHWEH El Hai (the living creator) shall see your Fast and great shall be your reward. Fast till Beelzebub (áòì œáåá - power of chaos, flies, death bringing), and all his evils depart from you, and all the angels of our Earthly Mother come and serve you. For I tell you truly, except you Fast, you shall never be free from the power of Satan and from all diseases that come from Satan. Fast and pray fervently, seeking the power of YAHWEH EL HAI ROPHENU, the living creator who heals, for your healing., while you Fast, stay away from people and seek our Earthly Mother's angels, for he that seeks shall find.*

Seek the Fresh Air of the Forest and of the Fields, and there in the midst of them shall you find the angel of air (Ruach EL). Take off your shoes and your clothing and suffer the angel of air to embrace all your body. Then breath long and deeply, that the angel of air may be brought within you. I tell you truly, the angel of air shall cast out of your body all uncleanness which defiled it without and within.

And then shall all evil smelling and unclean things rise out of you, like a smoke of fire rises upward and is lost in the ocean of air.
For I tell you truly, holy is the angel of air (Ruach El), who cleanses all that is unclean and makes evil smelling things of a sweet odor.

No man may come before the face of YAHWEH Elohim unless through the angel of air. Truly all must be born again by air and by truth, for your body breathes the air of the Earthly Mother, and your spirit breathes the truth of the heavenly Father. There are three things that bear witness: The spirit (Ruach) in helped (Breath, wind, spirit, air), the water and the blood; and these three agree in one. 1 John 5:4-8.

After the angel of Air, seek the angel of water (El Shamayim), take off your shoes and all your clothing and suffer the angel of water to embrace all your body. Cast yourself wholly into the water, as often as you move the air with your breath, move with your body the water also. I tell you truly, the angel of water (El Shamayim) shall cast out of your body all uncleanness which defiled it without and within. And all unclean and evil smelling things shall flow out of you, like the dirt that is in your clothing when it is washed, is cleansed, I tell you truly, holy is the angel of water (El Shamayim) who cleanses all that is unclean and makes all evil smelling things of a sweet odor. No man can come before the face of YAHWEH whom the angel of water lets not pass.

In Truth, all must be born again of water and of truth, for your body bathes in the waters of Earthly Life, and your spirit bathes in the waters life everlasting. For you receive your blood from our Earthly Mother and truth from our Heavenly Father.

Think not that it is sufficient that the angel of water embrace you outwards only, I tell you truly the uncleanness within is greater by much than the uncleanness without. And he who cleanses himself without, but within remains unclean, is like a tombs that outward are painted fair, but are within full of all manner of horrible uncleanness and abominations. So I tell you truly, suffer the angel of water to baptize you also within, that you may become free from all your past sins, and that within likewise you may become as pure as the flowing rivers sporting in the sunlight.

Take a large water bag that is used for a enema, fill it up with water from a river only, do not use tap water from faucet it must be water from Mother Earth that has not been polluted, hang the water bag up high placing the enema tube into your hinder parts, let the water flow through all your bowels. Afterwards rest kneeling on the ground for floor before the angel of water (EL Shamayim) and pray the angel of water that he will forgive you all your past sins, and pray the angel of water that will free your body from every uncleanness and disease. After this let the water run out from body, that it may carry away from within, it all the unclean and evil smelling things of Satan. I tell you, you shall see and smell all the foul smelling things that has tormented your body with all manner of pains. I tell you truly, baptism with water frees you from all of these. Renew your baptism with water on every day of your fast, till the day when you see that the water that flows out of you runs as pure as the river water.

Then baptize yourself in a river of water after seven days of Fasting, and give thanks to the angel of water and the heavenly Father for freeing you of your sins. This holy baptism is rebirth unto new life. For your eyes shall see and your ears shall here. Sin no more, after your baptism the angel of air and of water, may eternally abide in you and serve you forever.

And afterward if there remains within you aught of your past sins and uncleanness, seek the angel of sunlight. Take off your shoes and clothing and suffer the angel of sunlight to embrace all your body. Then breath long and deeply, that the angel of sunlight come within you. And the angel of sunlight shall cast out of your body all evil smelling and unclean things which defiled the body without and within. I tell you the truth, holy is the angel of sunlight who cleans out all uncleanness and make all evil smelling things of a sweet odor. None may come before the Face of YAHWEH Elohim whom the angel of sunlight lets not pass. Truly we must be born again of sun and Truth, for the body bakes in the sunlight of the truth of our Heavenly Father. The angels of Air and water and sunlight are brethren. They were created from the sons of man that they might serve him, and that he might go always from one to another. Holy likewise is there embrace. They are indivisible children of the Earth Mother, so do not put asunder those whom the earth and heaven had made one, let these three brother angel enfold you everyday and let them abide with you through all your Fasting.

For I tell you truly, the powers of devils, all sins and uncleanness shall depart from you in haste from the body which embraced by these three angel, As thieves flee from a house that has been left alone and the owner of the house returns, they flee one by the window the other by the roof, even so shall flee from your bodies all devils of evil, all past sins, and all uncleanness and diseases which defiled the temple of your bodies. When the Earthly Mother's angels enter into your bodies, in such wise that the El (power strength mighty) of your temple repossess it again, then shall the evil smell depart in haste by your breath and by your skin, corrupt waters by your mouth and by your skin, by your hinder and private parts. All these things you shall see with your eyes, smell with your nose and through your hands. And when all sins and uncleanness are gone from your body, your blood shall become as pure as a running river of water in the sunlight like the Earthly Mother's blood is pure. And your breath shall become as pure as the odor of flowers: your flesh as pure as flesh of fruits ripening upon the leaves of a tree: the light of your eyes as clear as bright as the sunlight.

And now shall all the angels of the Earth's Mother serve you and your breath, the blood and flesh of the Earthly Mother, that your spirit also may become one with the spirit of the heavenly Father. For truly no one can reach the heavenly Father unless through the Earthly Mother.

Even so, no newborn child can understand the teaching of this Father, until, his mother has suckled him, nursed him, nurtured him and put him to sleep, while the child is small his place is with his mother, and he must obey his mother. When the child is grown-up the Father takes him to work at his side in the field, and the child comes back to the Mother only when the hour of dinner and supper comes. Now his Father teaches him, that he might become skilled in the work of his Father. And when the

Father sees that his son understands his teachings and does his work well, he gives him all his possessions.

I tell you, truly happy is that son who accepts the counsel of his Father and Mother, for it was said to you: "Honor thy Father and thy Mother and keep all her laws, that they may prolong your days on this earth." But I say to you sons of man: Honor your Earthly Mother and keep all her laws, that your days may be long on this Earth, and Honor your Heavenly Father that Eternal Life may be yours in the heavens. For the Heavenly Father is a hundred times greater than the all the Fathers by seed and by blood, and greater is the Earthly Mother than all mothers by body on this earth.

For this is the True baptism that causes a man to be born again according to the Hebraic teaching of the Messianic Essene Order of Melchizedek.. Truth pressed down to the earth will one day rise again, and this is that day.   *Amen.*

THE LAST DAY PROPHECY OF MELCHIZEDEK FROM THE DEAD SEA SCROLLS

And concerning that He said, In this year of jubilee, each of you shall return to his property Lev. 25:13; and likewise, And this is the manner of release: every creditor shall release what he lent to his neighbor. He shall not exact it of his neighbor and his brother, for Elohim's release has been proclaimed. Dt. 15:2

And it will be proclaimed at the **end of days** concerning the captives, as he said: To proclaim liberty to the captives. Is 61:1 Its interpretation is that he will assign them to the Sons of Heaven and to the inheritance of Melchizedek; for He will cast their lot amid the portions of Melchizedek, who will return them there and will proclaim to them liberty, forgiving them, the wrong-doings of all their iniquities.

And this thing will occur in the first week of the jubilee that follows the nine jubilees. And the Day of Atonement is the end of the tenth jubilee, when all the Sons of Light and the men of the lot of Melchizedek will be atoned for. And a statute concerns them to provide them with their rewards. For this is the moment of the Year of Grace for Melchizedek. And he will, by his strength, judge the holy ones of Yahweh, executing judgement as it is written concerning him in the Songs of David, who said, Elohim has taken his place in the divine council; in the midst of the gods he holds judgement Ps 82:1. And it was concerning him that he said, (Let the assembly of the peoples) return to the heights above them, El (Power) will judge the peoples Ps 7:7-8. As for that which he said: How long will you judge unjustly and show partiality to the wicked? Selah Ps 82:2, its interpretation concerns Belial and the spirits of his lot, who were rebelled by turning away from the precepts of Yahweh to..... And Melchizedek avenge the vengeance of the judgments of Elohim.....and he will drag them from the hands of Belial and from the hands of all the spirits of this lot. And all the elohim of justice will come to his aid to attend to the destruction of Belial. And the height is...all the sons of Elohim...this.... This is the day of Peace/Salvation concerning which Yahweh spoke through Isaiah the prophet, who said, How beautiful upon the mountains are the feet of the messenger who proclaims peace, who brings good new, who proclaims salvation, who says to Zion: "your Elohim reigns Isa 52:7. Its interpretation: the mountains are the prophets... and the messenger is the Anointed one of the spirit, concerning whom Daniel said, Until an anointed one, a prince (Dan. 9:25)... And he who brings good news, who proclaims salvation: it is concerning him that it is written... To comfort all who mourn, to grant to those who mourn in Zion Isa. 61:2-3. To comfort those who mourn: its interpretation, to make them understand all the ages of time... In truth....will turn away from Belial...] by the judgments of Yahweh, as it is written concerning him, who says to Zion; Your Elohim reigns. Zion is..., those who uphold the covenant, who turn from walking in the way of the people. And Your Elohim is Melchizedek, who will save them from the hand of Belial.

As for that which He said, Then you shall send abroad the trumpet in all the land. Lev. 25:9.....

BIBLIOGRAPHY

Mathers, M. Kabbalah Unveiled. New York: Weisers, Inc. 1980

Charlesworth, James H. The Old Testament Pseudopigrapha, vol. I, Duke University, Doubleday and Company, Inc. 1983

Emmerson, Ralph Waldo. Selected Essays. New York: Penguin Books, 1982 Larzer Ziff, Editor

Robbins, Anthony. Unlimited Power. New York: Fawcett Publishing Group, 1987.

Hurtak, J. J. The Keys of Enoch. California. The Academy for Future Science. 1977

Urantia Foundation, The Urantia Book, Chicago, Illinois, 1978

Vermes, Geza, The Complete Dead Sea Scrolls in English, Penguin Books, London, England, 1997

250621-500-6-60W